T0117042

YOU ARE LOVE

Enrich Your Life Practicing Love and Loving
Ways and Contribute to Humanity

Mary LaSota

iUniverse, Inc.
New York   Bloomington

YOU ARE LOVE
Enrich Your Life Practicing Love and Loving Ways and Contribute to Humanity

iUniverse books may be ordered through booksellers or by contacting:

iUniverse
1663 Liberty Drive
Bloomington, IN 47403
www.iuniverse.com
1-800-Authors (1-800-288-4677)

Because of the dynamic nature of the Internet, any Web addresses or links contained in this book may have changed since publication and may no longer be valid. The views expressed in this work are solely those of the author and do not necessarily reflect the views of the publisher, and the publisher hereby disclaims any responsibility for them.

ISBN: 978-1-4401-6100-1 (pbk)
ISBN: 978-1-4401-6101-8 (ebook)

Printed in the United States of America

iUniverse rev. date: 8/13/09

To my friend, Loretta Hovey, who has lovingly helped me through many difficult times.

CONTENTS

I have been working with our beloved Archangel Raphael for several years now and was prompted to write this book by him. The ideas presented were given to me during prayer sessions with this very loving Archangel.

A FAMILY OF DIVINE LOVE

On earth there are so many definitions of love that it would fill volumes upon volumes of books to truly define love. Despite the many definitions, love is a challenge and sometimes even a mystery. The 1929 musical "Wake Up and Dream" had a hit song in it called, "What is This Thing Called Love?" written by Cole Porter. It was recorded by many of our well known artists. There is also a story attached to this song. Aliens visit Earth and take hostage two humans, a man and a woman. The aliens question the humans about human interaction and methods of human reproduction which are quite different from that of the aliens. The humans were said to be quite upset over the interrogation to the degree that the aliens returned the humans to earth. As the aliens return to their planet, the two humans fall in love.

Most movies, TV shows, and stage plays have a love story written into them. Love creates many feelings in us. In simple terms, love means deep caring for a special person. It can also mean fondness for a thing, such as, "I love my car," or "I love my snowmobile." Many individuals have bottomless feelings of love for their pets and refer to them in a loving way. Some even proclaim they love their pets more than their spouses or partners. We may love our friends, co-workers, those who have helped us in one way or the other. Love transcends all in life.

If we had no one to express this loving affection for, our lives would be dark, dismal, without purpose. Love adds drive to all situations. It sometimes gives us the will to move in a positive direction. It helps us recover from difficult times.

Many people describe love as a magnificent experience between two individuals which may lead to a permanent relationship including sexual love. Theologian Thomas Jay Oord concludes that love is a condition which allows us to act intentionally to encourage overall well-being.

In Sanskrit, the word Sat-Chit-Ananda is used to express the uniqueness of God. Sat means "being" which relates to God's eternal characteristics. Chit translates to "intelligence" which denotes God's creativity. Ananda generally means "bliss" which portrays God as peaceful, loving and always filled with happiness. It is important to reach out and experience God's love.

The Bible is clear in stating God is Love (1 John 4:8). We are automatically merged with him because he created us. So, in a very true sense, God's love for us is our love for the Divine God and all of humanity. Love of God is a vital concept in personal views about God. When we use the phrase, "Love of God," it can indicate the love God has for us or the love we have for the Divine God.

Love comes from God in the Christian viewpoint. The love of man and woman, eros in Greek, and the unselfish love of others, agape, are considered to be ascending and descending love. Agape is beautifully expressed in Thessalnians 3:12: "May the Lord make your love increase and overflow for each other and for everyone else." Many interpret this to mean charitability, altruistic and unconditional love for one another. It is with this love that goodness is created in our world. God loves all of humanity; Christians sometimes strive to have this love for one another. The word Phileo was also used in the New Testament along with Agape. Phileo is a pleasant type of love, as one would use for "brotherly love" or "sisterly love."

In Christianity, we turn once again to John 3:16-18,NIV which notes, "God so loved the world that he gave his one and only Son, that whoever believes in him shall not perish but have eternal life. For God did not send his Son into the world to condemn the world, but to save the world through him. Whoever believes in him is not condemned, but whoever does not believe stands condemned already because he has not believed in the name of God's one and only son."

The Disciple Paul also wrote, "Dear friends, let us love one another for love comes from God. Everyone who loves has been born of God and knows God. Whoever does not love does not know God, because God is love." (I John 4.7-8, NIV).

In Deus Caritas Est, translated from Latin to mean, "God is Love," is the encyclical composed by Pope Benedict XVI. The subject of this encyclical is Christian love. Eros and Agape are both good, but Eros is downgraded to sex when not steadied by elements of spiritual Christianity. The edict that Eros is inherently good follows the Catholic thought known as the "Caritas tradition", and is in contrast with the views expressed by a Lutheran bishop, Anders

Nygren. In his book, Agape is the only truly Christian type of love, and Eros deals with desires and turns away from God. These positions have been subject to debate by the Catholic and Protestant communities. The encyclical makes the argument that Eros and Agape are divided halves of complete love, and integrated by both giving and receiving.

There is a commonality amongst the religions that God is Love. Here are a few examples of this.

Taoism: The Supreme loves and nourishes all there is.

Buddhism: As the bright sun covers all regions, so does the God of Love protect and direct all human and animal life.

Christianity: God is Love, and he who abides in love abides in God and God lives in him.

Native American: Love is the authentic God of all the world.

Bahd't: Everything that isn't love is but words.

Krishna beliefs center on rasas, which deals with the emotional factors of our existence. Two faiths of Krishna worship each with its own system of philosophy.

Followers of Krishna worship according to their own tastes of worshipping their godhead. The followers of Krishnaism follow the deity of Krishna, oftentimes called the intimate deity, as compared with numerous four-armed forms of Narayana. It is complex, but there is a definite interaction between the love of God towards all of creation, the love of all of creation towards God and the relationship between the two.

In Mahayana Buddhism, the Bodhisattva involves renouncing oneself in order to take on the suffering of the world. The greatest motivator for this path of the

Bodhisattva is salvation, with unselfish love for all sentient beings.

Judaism has many definitions of love between man and Diety. The Torah states, "Love your neighbor like yourself." (Leviticus 19:18). With regard to loving God, there is this, "love God with all your heart, with all your soul and with all your might" (Deuteronomy 6:5). Ahava is the word used for love of God. Rabbi Eliyahu Eliezer Dessler defines love as "giving without expecting to take" (from his Michtav me-Eliyahu, Vol 1).

Kama is pleasurable love in Hinduism as personified by the God Kamadeva. This God is most often pictured holding a bow of sugar cane and flowers. He sometimes rides upon a great parrot. Kamadeva is usually accompanied by his consort Rati. Differing from Kama, Prema makes reference to elevated love. Karuna is empathy which reduces the suffering of others. A person who practices Bhaki gives devotion to the supreme God.

In the Islamic view, Allah is their God. There is also Al-Wadud, translated as "the loving one," which is found in Surah 85:14. This passage states God is "full of loving kindness." Each individual's effort determines to what degree that person has pleased God. Ishq, meaning divine love, is the importance of Sufism. Sufis worship that love which is an outcrop of God to the entire Universe. Sufism tends to see beauty in nature. It is often referred to as the religion of love. Sufi poetry oftentimes uses the word Beloved. Sufis believe that humankind can return to elegance.

Divine Love was important to Medieval German mystics. Women expressed Divine Love as a burning passion deep within the body.

Divine Love is the most beautiful love anyone can

experience. We have all experienced it. We were born with Divine Love in our physical self, soul, and heart. It all began in the celestial realms where we were between lifetimes. Or, it could be we were just beginning our first lifetime. There the clarity of Divine Love was ours as we were amongst Angels, Archangels, Ascended Masters, our Divine God, and others in the delightful realms. Our souls knew only too well the bliss of Divine Love, for there it is easier to understand for the soul.

The soul intermingled with all those in the celestial realms in an even and equal way. Spirit life is an exciting example of the ways in which our world can adapt to Divine Love. It was in the celestial realms that everyone loved, be it another soul, an angel, an Archangel, Ascended Master, or our Divine God in a way that love became prominent just as it was when our Divine God first created us. The longing to assist and help one another was always amongst the souls in their world; it was carried to the others who were in this perfect conclave of love which included both giving and receiving love.

It was here the soul first learned about love. Actually, it was the breath of our Divine God into each soul that made it possible for love to overcome the many situations that occur in the Divine heavens. This happens before a soul decides to come to earth. Others in the celestial realms may support one in a soul's plan.

Other souls or angels may be at the side of the soul in the waiting period between being in the celestial realms and coming back to earth. There may be questions and discussions a soul has about the uncertainty of life on earth. Other souls, guides, angels and our Divine God assist the soul in building a community of love in the higher realms. That community of love is so strong that no soul or anyone else in the heavens wants to do anything to break it or jeopardize its goodness and divineness. Here major plans are put together for a better world based on blueprints of tried ideals in the heavenly realms.

The love amongst those in the heavenly realms is so very strong that nothing can interfere with its mighty triumphs. They are distinctly the planners to bring such love to earth for they know that an individual's life would be greatly enriched by it. Archangel Raphael best uses the word Joy to indicate the ultimate love that may be reached on this our earthly planet. When we reach this ultimate state, our lives and the lives of all humankind will become enriched beyond comprehension. We will have then reached what he refers lovingly to as the ultimate, that which is Joy.

The soul is so capable of paving the way for absolute serene love which is built into all of us by our Divine God. It is strongly believed that all in the celestial realms carry the foundation for a life marked by the ultimate, that which is Joy. In the heavenly realms, all the souls and others work directly with our Divine God in keeping the celestial realms transparent with love in order that everyone may learn from each and every experience which occurs. It begs no difference! It is all based on love!

Those who remain in the celestial realms for long periods of time have many different duties to perform. The workings of the heavens are very much as the workings of the earth except in the heavens the plan of love unites everyone in A Family of Divine Love. All spirit life in the celestial realms realizes a close relationship to our Divine God and all others who are there. There is no doubt that the love existing in the celestial realms is the love our Divine God wants for those of us on earth. The celestial realms are constantly 'occupied' with spirit life; a measure would suggest they inhabit just as much space as life on our earthly planet. At times, this may fluctuate a bit as souls begin new lives on earth but the changes are not deemed to be at spectacular levels.

Many plans that souls make up during their stay in the celestial realms are very ambitious and tried out there. They evolve around current nows and future nows. Past 'nows' are not important but may at times be used only as reference material. When they seem to work to the fullest and love prevails in all instances, the soul feels there is hope of living their plan on earth to make our earth a better and more stable place for all humans filled with loving endeavors. Most plans work completely and it brings magnificence to a soul. The soul enters life with great expectations of achieving loving greatness and assisting humanity in this world of ours.

The heavenly realms may not look exactly like our towns and cities here on earth, nonetheless, heaven may simply be described as a paradise of untold and difficult to describe beauty and love energies. Besides the beauty that is divine, it is a situate of holiness. In a prayer session our beloved Archangel Raphael described the celestial realms as reflecting the greatest love possible. It is a kind of love that a human cannot even visualize nor comprehend. The heavens are miraculously made up of the love of our Divine God, the Ascended Masters, Archangels, Angels and others in the realms. A more powerful love cannot be experienced! This was stressed many times by Raphael. There is no physical mass in our heavens because, of course, souls do not need such an element. There are, however, many areas, each considered loving and sacred to the realms. Each such section serves a specific purpose for the soul and all others in the realms and is used wisely.

Love energy creates the beauty of lights, and the illumination reproduces all the time, making for a stronger energy. The energies of the heavens beam their light to earth so that humanity would consume it to make their existence better. These energies also guide us in all of our endeavors be they emotional or physical. Our Divine God, the greatest healer there is, discharges healing energies on our earth. At times these enormous energies of our loving Divine God are directed at humankind and sometimes at vegetable life, such as the crops we are to eat and enjoy.

Each soul may have as many angels, guides, and others from the realms as the soul delights to help and assist them. Our Divine God is always the giver of only the greatest love possible to each soul and everyone in the celestial realms. At times a soul may ask our Divine Creator for some sort of change which will help them produce results on earth. Our Divine God cooperates one hundred percent with each soul and offers only loving suggestions. Souls love being in the heavenly realms as much as the Angels, Archangels, Spirit Guides, and others, and our Divine God. It is something all of us aspire to even now in our daily lives on earth.

It is definitely a give and take atmosphere in the celestial realms. The soul learns from the Angels, others, and our Divine God, and they learn from their Soul. Oftentimes, if a Soul has had many lifetimes on earth there is a lot to offer those who want to come and have had only one incarnation. Also, the Soul can be of great benefit to an Angel who wants to come to earth and serve humankind, especially if it is the Angel's first undertaking. Angels are created by our Divine God all the time. Our Divine God believes in a large family of love both here on earth and in the celestial realms. It is our Divine God's one loving desire to combine those in both kingdoms in A Family of Divine Love.

Angels who wish to come to earth also make up comprehensive plans of goodness they wish to bestow on the many. They believe strongly beyond any doubt that earthly life can and will some day be a cherished life fundamentally filled with the love of the Ages. They want to teach, yes, teach love to all humans. They only want happiness, love, and enrichment for all human life and this includes animal life and all other life as well. For how we personally feel has a direct bearing on how much love we give to our pets. The manner in which we pat our pets reflects love. The way in which we give them their daily or weekly bath reflects this. The approach we use in calling them and speaking to them reflects how much love we have for them. Our pets are sensitive creatures by nature, all of them, and they pick up on this. If we are loving with them, they give back to us tenfold and sometimes even more.

The love with which we grow our gardens also reflects the love within the deepness of our hearts. When we take the time to dig up the soil ourselves, if our garden is of fair size, it shows the love we have for the soil. When we kneel down afterwards and take the beautiful dark soil into our hands and bless it in our own loving way, the soil will respond to this treatment and we will be abundantly rewarded.

Simple prayer words like:

Divine God, Archangel Raphael, and everyone in the celestial realms, I ask that

what I plant grows with the greatest quantity.
May it be sweet to my taste, and that of my
loved ones and others who will
consume it
Amen

Whatever prayer words are used for this purpose are just fine.

When we remember to water our plants when there is a lack of rain from nature, the plants will react. If we are filled with a deep, giving love, the fruits and vegetables we grow will reflect this, as we and those who partake in the food we grow will be healthier and in some cases it may even alleviate certain illnesses. Growing a garden will not be a chore but a loving experience. If we have extra space and a neighbor wants to utilize this space to grow vegetables, we will lovingly offer him or her that space. After having watched us work on our garden in a loving way, there's a chance that individual will do the same.

At the time the food is ready to be picked from your loving garden, just stand there for many moments looking at the vegetables. Tell yourself how beautiful they are. If you are a first-time grower, tell yourself how well you did! Then, after due fashion, pick the vegetables. You will want to wash them and when they are in your hands being washed, say the following:

Divine God, thank you for these
spectacular vegetables which my family
and I will consume. Growing vegetables
has helped me travel on my spiritual path
in a loving way.
Amen

Your own words will do as well.

Lastly, after you cook your vegetables and you are about to consume them, you will actually feel a bit excited about it. Something will come to your mind like, "Wow, these vegetables are going to taste so good!" When you and those with you begin to eat your meal, you will find this to be true.

As you know, spirit life has no gender until it comes to earth and is born. Then it is gender the soul asked for in their plan, believing it would accomplish the most for all humans and humankind in particular.

There are those times, too, when a soul returns to the celestial realms after a life on earth and is very unhappy. Their life on earth was not a joyous one but rather one filled with unsolvable problems, anxiety, pressures, hatred, and anger. This was in no way the soul's fault, but this type of soul needs an extraordinary amount of love and receives it from everyone in the celestial realms it comes into contact with. Slowly, the soul rehabilitates but may not want to go back to earth for many years.

As our lives began to unfold, there were many twists and turns in our road of life which may have somehow changed our hopes, beliefs and aspirations for ourselves. Our Divine God tries to make a compatible match between our plans for our lives and those we are born to. The situation is so complicated because at times the lives of our parents unravel and our physical self and soul is left in a quandary. Take the case of divorce in a household. The child feels different from before. Even though both parents may indicate that closeness will always remain, it is not certain the child believes it. In some cases, this does not occur, further departing from a plan which was engineered in heaven.

In another case, a child is born to a single mother and there is such love between them. The child is happy but not for long. The single mother may find a partner she loves very much and the partner moves into their household. Getting used to a father figure is difficult for the child, and there is the feeling that this man means more to the mother than the child does. There is such stress put upon a child in these cases. The stress lasts unless it is dealt with. In most instances the child is afraid to discuss feelings with the mother, thinking the mother only cares for her partner.

There is no judgment in the higher realms and so the soul takes on whatever duties will enhance as much love as possible to the soul. All those in the celestial realms play a blissful part in this process. The soul once again finds itself, for it thrives on love. When a soul 'fills' with love, it is happily and joyfully noticed by those in the heavens.

In the celestial realms there is no such thing as making a mistake about an issue. There is no blame attached to anyone. So often one hears that Angels are just too perfect, and it's hard to believe such perfect beings exist. If truth be known, Angels and all others in the celestial realms undergo situations. They are perhaps different occurrences in their very nature, but the major difference between those in the celestial realms and some humans is the manner in which these occurrences are handled. All in the celestial realms handle every situation which may occur with love. It is a simple model yet one which works beyond reason or explanation. That is why their energies are always so healing and rewarding for humans.

Divine love is the love of heaven and earth. It is the love which every soul receives directly from God. It is the same love which the Divine God has given to all those in the heavenly realms. It is a love with which all matters may be handled in a calm and peaceful manner for a loving resolution. God's Divine Love is within our hearts, souls, and bodies.

It is this proximity with the Divine Spirit which asks for nothing from us. Divine love is that love which will enrich our lives while we are on this earth and at the same time do something of relevance for humanity. It is that love which carries over to the afterlife where we plan our next incarnation learning from previous ones. Divine love is the love between all those in the angelic realms, the earth, and our Divine God. We are all a part of A Divine Family of Love.

The Loving Physical Self

The physical body may be described as an energy mass which occupies time and space for a given duration of time. The physical body is made up of necessary organs and tissues and houses a spiritual component. Psychologists point out that the physical body is an object with physical properties. Some behaviorists believe a physical body, including its properties, are the only important matter of experimentation and study.

Philosophers claim a physical body is a concrete physical object and exists in the world of physical space. In most philosophies, the physical body is not a mental object in a mental world nor is it an abstract object as proposed in the world of Platonic concepts. Emotions most definitely are not considered to be physical bodies.

In Theosophy, a form of mysticism, the physical body is referred to as the last progressively denser vehicle of consciousness. Blavatskyian Theosophy calls the body sthula sarira or the gross body which is distinguished from the linga sarira, subtle body.

In new age philosophies, the physical body is contrasted with spirit. It houses spirit and the body is left behind in ascension into heaven. In many New Age philosophies, a physical body is in contrast with the spirit, soul or heavenly body. It is a home for the soul which is left behind at the time of death.

You are love! This is a beautiful statement and it's true. All human beings on this our earthly planet are love. Our beloved Archangel Raphael ends his messages with this beautiful affirmation. At times, he will give an answer to a question in thought form to an individual, never forgetting to say those magical words of truth. If something is bothering us, he may find a way to show us the answer out of our dilemma and make us feel better by telling us we are love. When healing of our physical body is needed, Archangel Raphael is there for us with love that spreads throughout our physical body. The Angelic healer, as he is known in the celestial heavens, and in the Universe as a whole, will not ever let us down and he will never stop telling us that we are indeed love.

The physical self lacks permanence. Our physical bodies are often overstretched further than their normal range. It's the physical self, the body, which suffers when overburdened. When the body is unable to perform that which it was meant to, it is necessary for us to reload it. We each may have a different way of doing this. Some of us may go dancing. To others, a movie is relaxing. Still others may have lunch or dinner with a friend or friends. Some of us enjoy our hobby. Very few of us will sit in a comfortable chair and tell ourselves we are love and as such much is possible for us. We forget to ask our angels to help us get through a problematical time of our life. We seek help by allowing ourselves 'artificial' means of healing through this world's material things, which in a sense may be helpful in the short run. We fail to recognize that which is helpful in the long run and that is love of physical self.

In simplistic terms, our physical bodies are composed of necessary organs for life such as lungs, liver, stomach, pancreas, and tissues. In addition to the organs, muscles, and tissues are the emotional concerns. It is important to recognize that each individual has a psychological, physical and spiritual component. There are various schools of thought, and it is not our mission to go into detail about them here.

However, we will mention a few. Some believe the physical self is a physical object with physical properties. Others think it's something of a concrete nature which exists in and is absolute in the physical world of physical space. In some systems of mysticism, the physical self is considered to be the last of the thicker vehicles of awareness.

Each and every one of us as Beings of love has a definite purpose for our existence. Within this pattern of purpose there is enormous love interwoven into it. It is also the love which may flow from one person to the next until the Earth is filled with the purity of it. This was an idea our Divine God had when he created us and our loving earth.

Archangel Raphael has a history of believing in us, and that is why he constantly reiterates the phrase "You Are Love". If you believe it, all you desire will be possible for you. And, too, if you believe it, the Universe will be a loving place. It will be a place filled with love as all humans would be participants in this undertaking. I will most likely keep telling you throughout this book that You Are Love as that's what Archangel Raphael wants me to do.

Angels are celestial beings close to the Divine yet

they themselves had ordeals to go through to prove to the Divine God that they were worthy of the honor bestowed upon them.

They want us to understand this! Archangel Raphael has many stories to tell which would fill a thousand books. Yet, in each and every case, the profoundness of Raphael is love. He knows and may explain to us through his teachings what "You are love" really means. He believes all things are possible through and with love. We are not talking about sexual love here. Nor, are we referring to love one has for a spouse, partner, family member, friend or the like.

The love Archangel Raphael refers to is a love which comes directly from God given to us by God. We in return may look at it as a love of self and all of humanity which makes it possible for us to have that which we desire most to enrich our lives. But, unless we include all Beings in our love process, we are missing our goal and mission of our existence on this beautiful earthly planet.

Each and every Being on our earthly planet is love! The energy of those tender words is at all times exceedingly prevailing. There is a definite sentiment that there are too many Beings who don't really accept the truth as it is.

It is a fact that all humans want to feel this love, yet there are distinct reasons why some will not allow themselves to. The actual explanation is directly related to the lack of enthusiasm for the spiritual and a pessimism which grew through the generations from thousands of years gone by to the present now.

Belief systems are deeply ingrained within us.

There are countless added reasons which stop us from believing that we are love. It may be due to an individual's formidable early years and teachings, hurtful life experiences, the inability of one person to understand another person, peer pressure, a devastating relationship and a lack of a definite want. And, too, high on the list is our unfair class system which most of us struggle within all our lives.

As we all recognize, the Universe is in a beautiful transformation in this current now. We are coming upon an era of existence which will be more meaningful to all humans. It will allow us the opportunity to give to others our words and actions to create a better world. There will be a resurrection of those great days gone by where love answered all, even the most difficult all.

Consider this a time of spectacular happenings! It may be referred to as a revolution back to love in heart, physical body and soul. As this occurrs, we humans want to participate in all activities whether minor or major. We want to give the best we can to accentuate that which is important in our lives here on Earth. We all have so much to offer. The selfishness we have seen has dissipated into the heavens and it is gone forever. The reluctance of our mission to help others is gone. We want to do all we can not only for those close to us but for all of humankind all over the world. It is a unique feeling when one realizes one is indeed love.

It seems like there's an offer on the table for everyone. It's a brilliant time which the likes of many haven't seen for thousands of years, yet is most fitting that this time return to all of us because it seems we are ready for it! We will peacefully and gently become our true unique physical self as our hearts rejoice to its merriment.

Creative thoughts will be accessible to those who reach out in true devotion. It is every day of one's existence as an individual and inhabitant of this planet that will fuel the best in us. It is all sacred and holy to a degree because this is what we have initially planned and intended to experience. There will be no longing for anything worth less than anything else. All symbolized dreams remain a part of the plan and are attainable in a Universe of love where the heart is prominent and always shall remain that way and where love dominates the physical self and soul.

All people want to believe that they are love. All inhabitants of our loving and beautiful Earth find this to be true if we allow it to be so. It was so when we first came to earth and there are many reasons why this precious love was in a sense lost. The Angels, together with Archangel Raphael and our Divine Lord will help us to regain this special love. For through the love of the ages, perfected love such as once endured, will be set in a framework of rich purification. There are ways to get back that which was lost the moment you came out of the womb and began interacting with others. Each will retain and acknowledge that which was received: this remarkable love. Present life will be filled with treasured love and everyone will possess an abundance to offer others assistance and love to work towards a common goal of oneness and Joy.

Joy is accessible in this lifetime of ours. It is meant to be for everyone. Joy is part of the special love of our physical body and soul. Our Divine God wants nothing less for us all.

Everyone deserves to once again find the sanctuary of healing, love and spiritual giving. It will not be difficult for all who want it, and returning to it will be a huge exhilaration of correctness like nothing no one on this earthly planet has ever observed.

The time is in this now for a new world to emerge. It has been in the closet for so many thousands of years. Maybe some here now shone light so bright that others here haven't ever forgotten about it. Some individuals were the ones who lived and created all the love necessary so many years ago. They lived then and are here now. It was as if a force of love exuded from your physical bodies and covered everyone and everything.

There are some things to acknowledge in this current now in order that each individual reaches the potential to love, the way they loved during the time many thousands of years ago. Doesn't it make for happiness to know that it can be so? That it is the time now to be free and filled with love which is the highest treasure the Divine meant for us all. And that happens to be love of the physical so deep, clear, sincere, that it is felt in your heart, the same as it was for the inhabitants who lived so many years ago. Your heart rings with happiness each moment! Yes, it is possible to regain the God given creative love of the physical body.

Those of you who are on this Earth now and were then in different incarnations surely recall the details of the most glorious and exquisite time when a person's light shone brightly with the Divine's light, and it reached the hearts of others in droves. Those who were here do remember the positive energy which in itself made things possible. And, this love energy flooded the air, buildings, common places, animals, vegetations and of course human life. There were many who lived during that celebrated magnificent time and are here again. Some are wondering what has happened over the years, expecting life to be the way it was then. They are disappointed, and this obviously has a direct effect on their living in this day and age. Others, also wondering what happened, ask themselves, "why this difference?" They weren't ready for a dramatic change of these proportions. They make a vow to try to change things that will have a swift return back to the days where pure love mattered. Some become very disgruntled and don't even want to be here and the consequences of these people are indeed sorrowful.

It is important to say here also that some who were living then and are here now are happy. They simply adjusted to the way of the world and are trying to carry out the details of their plan. We must begin with the premise stated all along that our physical self is total, pure, beautiful love because it was given to us by our Divine Creator, God.

Based on this premise, it seems that now is a great opportunity to ride the wave and bring about the splendor of love to our lives in this current now.

There are no limits! All it takes is to recognize and be awakened to it, and some of you already are. Others need just a little push to become awakened to the greatness of love and why love plays the all important part in all of life and existence. It is important to note that everyone in oneness can bring this about. Like a newborn child who comes to earth with total love in body and soul, every individual may regain this special love. .

Joy is something our beloved Archangel Raphael describes as living an enriched life and helping others, utilizing love and loving ways. So, Joy is the goal we all want to strive for! A love of our Divine God, all humankind, the animal kingdom and all of nature will guide you through the steps of awareness until you find your total self immersed in love.

If one listens carefully the Joy of the world may be felt in the hearts of everyone because you are descendants of those who lived in the great bygone days. There is one important aspect to echo over and over again, and that is everyone, every human being on this earth, is just plain love. No one can reiterate differently for it isn't so. The adage that one person is love and another is not is just not true. We are all love because of our oneness with the Divine God and all those in the celestial realms, including those souls who are there resting before they begin a new life on Earth.

Everyone belongs to the brotherhood and sisterhood, whichever they have chosen, which breeds only total love. To characterize it into simple terms, this love leads to Joy. This Joy, or the greatest enrichment of life, is available to all. So much has transpired through the ages that an awakening of the truth is necessary. It's as if you were asleep living a virtual lie and now you have the opportunity to be your true self, the self that you wanted before coming to earth. The awakening may come in different fashion depending on you. It may come softly, or with great rumbling. The awakening clearly means that your physical self will once again experience total love, pure love, as it was meant to.

In this current now, this awakening may happen and wouldn't that be a marvelous day? Like the light of the Divine God and celestial beings, your light would be bright to designate the bliss you are feeling in anticipation of the awakening. And when the awakening took place, what an astounding experience it would be.

It is important at this juncture to ask yourself the question of whether or not the time for awakening is right for you. When you came to earth, the time was right. As tiny and holy as you were then, you came with awakening and a great flash of light surrounded your little body. Your first breath was that of awakening as you cried out in heavenly Joy. Your little body wanted to participate in a life of enrichment where you would help others, and others would help others, and the line would go on in a oneness paradigm. This was your real intention as you drew up your map for living before entering this Earthly planet. But many things happened along this beautiful course to change your original hallowed intentions. Some of you, however, were able to maintain the special love given to you by our God. It is recognizable through your loving spiritual accomplishments and love for humankind.

It is well to remember that you are the light, and it is through this brilliant light that you stand out. All perceived inadequacies are wiped away. All the dreariness of your world is wiped away, leaving and filling your physical self with Joy based on the love of the centuries. This should always make you feel good that you have the courage to regain the lost love. The love of your physical self, or part of that love, was lost due to circumstances and the manner in which the world operates in this particular now. We see much animosity, hatred, jealousy, abuse, selfishness, to mention only a few negativities.

All that you are, your experiences, are reason for your physical self to be filled with love. That is really the first step and you must think of it in that way. Some may think that if an experience was not pleasant it leaves a mark of some sort. That is the furthest from the truth.

Every experience makes your physical self more loving. Even the most difficult experience in life fills one's physical self with a love as you never imagined it would. It is these experiences that allow you to become a teacher to help and assist others who are doubtful in reaching their goal. So, life experiences are very important in the process we refer to as You Are Love.

There are those who may believe that it is only positive experiences that will fill your physical being with love. This is untrue. Experiences are what they are. They may be labeled as good or bad by some, yet, in true reality they are experiences from which the learning process occurs to assist others. If we truly believe this, as those who lived thousands of years ago did, it will help us achieve our goal.

In the goodness of life, we also want to remember that every child born on a certain day of a certain year as designated by the calendar, is filled with love, both physical and that of the soul. When you come to earth your love is overflowing in you and your soul because that's what was planned by you. It is through interactions with others, those who have been here for years, that you, the lovely child, begins to change. Suddenly, you begin to take on actions, thoughts, feelings of those around you and those who are assigned to care for you in your early years. This contributes to the looseness of love, and the most important love is retired. You get to love your parents. Later on, you get to love friends, a spouse, a partner and list goes on, but it is a different love. It is a strong love to be sure, but it is a love which creates the discourse from which you hesitate to learn. Instead, there are times of blame, hatred, jealousy, and other such attributes. These attributes only lead to other unpleasantries, and issues become deplorable. The love our Divine God breathed would not ever create such attributes for it is not possible to with love and loving ways.

It is very important to know who you are! This you know at birth and this must not ever be forgotten. but if it is. as it most likely is, in the current now we live in, it may be recaptured and the true nature of love reestablished. You must constantly tell yourself, "I am love! I am love!" You must believe it! There must be no jealousy attached to love.

It is important that you recognize each human to be love as well. So, it is necessary to say to yourself when you see a family member or another loved one, "You are love! We are love!"

This is the first step to a beautiful communion of gathering up the love of the ages and accepting it as your own because you were born with an enriching love. If you do it, it will bring you Joy. And, at the same time, others will be on a path to happiness.

Try to consider each life experience as just that. True, some may be more taxing than others. There are some which may change one's life forever. A good example of this is losing a loved one or loved ones.

I can personally attest to this. I came from a large loving family. I had two sisters and four brothers. My mother was an exceptionally giving woman. She was of Polish descent and came to this wonderful country when only fifteen. At that time she didn't know any English whatsoever and had to get by with the little knowledge of English she acquired from others on a day-to-day basis working in a fabric factory. At first when she arrived in our little town, mom lived with my aunt, but my aunt told her it would be only for a short time. She would need to find another place. So, mom moved into a boarding house, not far from the factory where she worked. She didn't mind living there because her meals were given to her and when she arrived home to the boarding house after a mean day's work all she wanted to do was eat supper and to go to sleep. When my mom made a little money, her loving heart opened as wide as it could, and Mom sent money to her family in Poland to help them out. She always remarked how good her total being felt when she was able to help her family.

My mom always wanted to become a doctor. When I was old enough to understand this, I felt so sorry for her that the dream she dreamt the most on those cold New England nights was not realized. You will know why this was not possible by the time you finish reading this segment. As I write this, I am crying for my Mom who I miss so very much for her goodness, charity, help, and most of all love. "Mom, I am so sorry you never became a doctor! You would have made a great doctor! You showed such compassion and love for humanity." But, the plan Mom designed for herself in the celestial realms maybe didn't include her desire to become a doctor. Even though Mom never formally studied medicine, she did much to educate herself by reading all kinds of material, including medical books.

My father was strict with all of us, yet there was a side of him we adored. He loved all of us kids. Despite the noise we siblings made constantly with our quarrels and disagreements, my dad put up with us. He tried to instill in us the importance of learning.

Dad was of German-Polish descent, and he was already in this country when my mom had arrived here. He was about nine years older than mom. They had met at the factory where both of them worked.

At first mom and dad were only friends, but mom told us dad liked her from the first moment they met. He would walk her home after work, and they would spend time talking about the 'old country' as they lovingly called it. They had so much in common, it seemed, but mom was so very young. She was too young to get serious about anyone. Mom was very sophisticated. It showed at an early age. She read so very much and took courses when she could. She was highly intelligent. Yet, under the circumstances, she felt protected by my dad who was older.

When mom was only sixteen, she and Dad married. With the little money they each had saved, Mom and Dad decided to see more of America and perhaps relocate to another area of the country where there might be more opportunity. Their travels took them South, and North, and West, and though they loved to travel and see new things,they found very much discrimination against foreigners. They decided to return to the small town where they lived before. So, they came back home to their friends and started a family. Mom and dad had seven children.

Dad loved to walk, and living in a small New England town as we did, it was fun taking a walk every Sunday. I still remember it today. We dressed very appropriately, in what we called our Sunday outfits, for church. After church, we would enjoy a freshly cooked dinner. Our dinners together were really something as Mom was a great cook! No one could equal her cooking abilities. We usually had chicken, stuffing and all the rest of it, topped off with strawberry shortcake or homemade strawberry pie. After that, Mom would always instruct us to change up as we had to be careful with our clothing, not to get it soiled. Then, Dad and I would go for a walk. If there were folks sitting on their porches, we would stop, and dad loved to talk to them.

A few of his male friends living in this town were dear to him as all of them came to this country at about the same time. Naturally, we would visit one or two of them and then head back home. As we walked dad always taught me a few words of Polish. He wanted me to know about my grandparents, whom I never saw because of the miles between us, but I knew a lot about them anyway. I remember dad telling me my grandfather had an orchestra and played at all the local events. Maybe that's why I like music so much! When I got home after one of these walks I was generally dog-tired, being the little kid I was at the time, and just flopped on my bed and went to sleep.

The first loss my family suffered was the death of my father from stomach and lung cancer. He was in his early fifties when it happened. My mom was still in her forties. Being the youngest in the family, I was just six years old. My mother was devastated. There were so many worries. Would she be able to keep the house my parents worked so hard for? Salaries were low in those days, and they counted pennies and nickels to pay the bills, mortgage and taxes. How would she support the children who were still at home? The doctor advised her not to go to work because of health problems. Having so many children, she needed a hysterectomy, too. Her belief that our Divine God loved her helped her through this difficult ordeal. My mom showed all of us kids love, and I do truly believe she was able to handle situations with love and loving ways. I noticed this about Mom, and it had a great bearing on my life. I wanted to be like Mom, calm, loving and serene!

My father's death had a tremendous impact on my life too. "My dad is gone and he'll never come back," I kept on telling myself. It was tough in school, too, as all the children would speak of their dad and, when it came for me to do so, I shyly said, "my dad died." I had no one to take me to the games like the other kids did. There wasn't a father to take me to the father-daughter school events either.

I cried when I was alone but never told any of my family about it. I wanted to be strong with them. I realize now it would have been a lot better if I opened up and told them how I felt. Instead, shyness seemed to creep in, and

I played it strong as if it was inevitable that my dad died. When alone, I cried and cried until my face was red and my eyes looked bloodshot! I spoke less, and the elders in the family labeled me as shy.

I couldn't even bring myself to publicly cry at dad's funeral! It was that ethic, "be strong!" Now, I wished I had cried to show him how much I loved him. And, how much I missed him and what a beautiful man he was for a girl to have as a dad! I didn't express emotion! I was like a stone with horrible disbelief, anger, and even hatred that my dad was taken away from the family. I now frequent his grave and cry loudly. My mom is buried in the same plot with my brother, Walt, there too. Just a little away at the next graveside is my dear sister, Fran, and her husband, Stan.

The next one to pass was my brother Ted. He was only thirty-eight when he died from a liver malfunction. Ted was in the military, and following that, he and his wife made their home in Hawaii, Guam, and subsequently in California. We saw Teddy and his loving wife probably only once a year, but the family got very excited about it. We all prepared when we knew Ted and his wife were to visit us. Teddy was the type who everyone liked. He touched the hearts of many with his kind, positive ways, and he would never refuse to do a favor for anyone if asked. For a time he worked for the CIA but then as an engineer on a road construction project in Guam. His stories were many, and the family was intently interested in his work as an engineer. As I look back, I realize Teddy always managed to do some loving act for someone whether or not he knew them.

The last time he and his wife visited us, he did tell my mom of a liver problem, but it didn't sound serious. When Teddy died, it was shocking news to all of us. I looked up to him as the 'perfect' big brother who did so much in his short life. My mom tried to keep her grief intact, but I knew what she went through. She lost Teddy, who was so good to her in so many ways! It was difficult for her to pull through this, but being a strong Polish woman, she did! I always believed, and still do, that you can judge a man by how he treats his mom. Teddy earned an A plus for the way he loved and treated Mom.

My mom was the next to leave us. She suffered one heart attack and then about three years later, a second one which took her. By then I was already working. Mom loved the movies. Even when she was the busiest with the kids, every Sunday she and some of the kids went to a movie with her. Dad didn't much care for movies and stayed home with the other kids. She also enjoyed theater in the round in the summer months, where great musicals were produced, and, of course, the New York stage. We lived about three hours away from New York by train, and often my brother, my mom, and I found ourselves in New York for weekends.

I missed my mom very much because she was such a loving woman who deeply cared not only for her family but those around her. I grieved silently for at least two years as I now recall. Life was just not the same without her. Some people will tell you, "life moves on; just go and have a good time. There's nothing you can do about it anyhow."

Grieving is an individual's right. Some persons may grieve one day; others two or three or five years.

My sister, Joan, a nurse, passed next. She was the oldest of the girls in the family. She worked in a large local hospital for many years. Joan had breast cancer and tried to hide it until she became so ill that it was necessary for her to call an ambulance to get to a nearby hospital. They performed surgery and removed her breast, but by then the cancer had already spread to other parts of her body. She suffered terribly, and our hearts were heavy in sorrow.

There were several years of peace. Maybe our Divine God gave us this gift in preparation for the losses to come. I lost three brothers and a sister within the framework of two years.

My brother, Al, the eldest of the boys had heart problems. In addition, his vision began to go. He was a chemical engineer, and it could be that working with chemicals   caused this loss. Even though he was married and had his own family, my eldest sister and he were very close. When Joan became ill, he suffered a first heart attack. After her death, he was devastated! Later on, he needed heart surgery. He was put on a respirator and lived only two to three weeks more.

My brother, Walt, loved to write and paint landscapes. He was also good at photography and enjoyed it as a hobby. Outdoor work like mowing the lawn, planting trees, flowers, and shrubs always gained his keen interest, and he had vigorously studied about nature. He worked as an accountant for many years, and later on, took care of Mom when she no longer could do for herself. The family pledged that we would always find a way to care for mom and not put her in a nursing home. This was her wish and it was followed with reverence.

Walt was very active, exercised, watched his weight and diet through the years. One day he began bleeding from the colon. I took him to the emergency room of the hospital and they kept him in the hospital for several days. The doctor who was going to perform a colonoscopy on him decided not to do it even though he was already prepped for it. Instead, he let him go home. About a week later, the bleeding began again during the middle of the night.

When we arrived in the emergency room, several tests were taken, including an ultra sound. It was determined he had a tumor and surgery was necessary. The surgery for colon cancer did not go well at all. He was kept in the hospital for the amount of time the insurance allowed. My brother's doctor wanted him to go to a nursing home for rehabilitation but instead he came home. He was very sick when he came home. At the same time, I had to have surgery to remove my ovaries.

I felt very uneasy leaving him alone but it was necessary for me to go to the hospital for my own surgery. My sister came to stay with him. While I was in the hospital, the message kept drumming into me over and over again that my brother was going to die. They gave me medication to put me to sleep but during that time, that's all my mind was telling me. After my surgery was over, they kept me in the hospital for several hours. After a long while, they released me, as everything went well for me. I kept thinking about my brother again and that he was going to die. Later, my nephew and sister came to take me home. They didn't say anything to me except a few pleasantries. When we got home, I felt very weak from the surgery, nevertheless happy to be home. It was then that my sister and nephew sat by me and told me Walt had passed away.

I must admit I felt very uneasy the entire time I was in the hospital for my surgery. I knew that something was going to happen to Walt. It was as if the angels, and particularly our beloved Archangel Raphael, were trying to prepare me for his death. At first I wasn't able to cry! I was weak from my own surgery and by the next morning, when I tried to get out of bed, I nearly passed out. My sister, Fran, was there for me. Somehow, with Divine help, I got through the funeral.

Approximately six months later, my brother, John, passed away. All my brothers were in the service of their country and proud to have served. John was especially proud because he was in the Marines. He loved being a Marine and took pride in telling everyone he was a Marine. Somehow, John believed being a Marine was the most honorable way a person could serve their country. My other brothers took it in stride as they were all in the Army. John was wounded while in combat. When he came home John refused to ask the government for a pension that was due him. He always said he served his country and that was pension enough.

John was very outgoing and people loved him. He also had a tremendous sense of humor. I remember some of the hilarious stories he told when I was a little girl. There was never a time when one of his stories didn't garner a laugh. Upon returning home from the Marines he married and had a little boy of his own. He loved his little boy with the deepness of his heart.

John loved fishing, hunting, gardening, and just being one with nature. He spent many an afternoon on a day off just walking in the woods. It happened slowly. John's appetite began to go. We were quite worried about him. Even though he maintained a regular regimen of checkups with his doctors, apparently this evaded them. He was sent to a large city hospital for tests. By then, he could barely walk, and his son had to practically carry him to the car. Shortly thereafter, John, his wife and son found out that he had liver cancer, which had already spread to the lungs. He refused chemotherapy as John knew he would soon die. It was about two weeks later, in fact, that he did die.

My sister, Fran, and I were the last ones left. I was the youngest of the family, and Fran, my dear sister, was the second oldest.

It was about six months after John died that Fran's breathing wasn't right. I remember getting a call from her. I took her immediately to the emergency room. They did many tests and took x-rays. The x-rays showed she had emphysema and it was already at an advanced stage.

My sister, like my mom, was a sophisticated, intelligent woman. She had owned and operated a beauty shop in a nearby town for about thirty five years and was a very successful business woman. She loved traveling. Fran and her husband traveled all over the world. She also loved art work and won several first prizes for some of her art work. Fran and her husband loved the outdoors, too, and spent time on their boat, or went blueberry picking in the woods, where it took hours upon hours to fill a pail of wild blueberries. Fran was respected by everyone, professionally and personally.

Her biggest regret in life was that she and her husband didn't have children. Fran compensated by being very compassionate and loving to the children in her neighborhood. They loved her for it! Sometimes, she would spend more money for grocery items for the kids than she would for herself. Fran had a heart of gold with everyone she touched. My big sister! I loved her so much! I will miss her so much! I kept telling myself this as I visited her each day, either in the hospital, at rehab or in her home. The emphysema kept getting worse and she suffered dreadfully. I felt so bad. Even during those difficult times she had, there were those who took advantage of Fran's giving and loving nature. Fran worried about me! She told me so! I guess Fran knew what was awaiting me!

Fran died!

There are two reasons for my telling just a little of my personal story. It is not because I am looking for tea and sympathy.

I was alone! I felt so alone! The big loving family was gone. There was just myself left. It was cruel for me to be so alone! Although I had wonderful loving friends, it just isn't like family. I had so many noble memories of all of them, but nevertheless I was left alone!

I thought about it for the longest time. Then, the Angels, and particularly, Archangel Raphael, helped me to understand that there was a reason for their passing when they did, and it wasn't so that I would be alone. It was because each had a mission or plan when they came into this magnificent world. Their plan had been completed and they were ready to return to the heavens to draw up another plan for a new incarnation. Although I will always miss and love them, understanding helps to heal and move on.

The second reason I had for telling this story was to show the love that was exuded in our family. It was a love which my mom and dad received from our Divine God and gave to us. We lived that love on nearly a daily basis. It was most noticeable during gatherings at the family home like Easter, Thanksgiving, or Christmas. One felt the loving energy in the room we were in, which eventually would reach out and fill the entire house. My parents gave us children a most wonderful gift by showing us through their own actions that love such as we had amongst ourselves could be categorized as a Divine Love.

A deep love on a physical level which you were supplied with when you came to Earth is something that stays with you. It is very much related to soul, which we will talk about a little later. The physical level of unhappiness is shown to most of us through pain, difficulties of one sort or another, unhappiness, anger, and emotional unsteadiness.

Emotional unsteadiness will wipe away the love we are talking about. Therefore, it is most necessary to keep oneself in constant evenness in all situations. If we do acknowledge the fact that one situation has equal value to another situation, it will be so much easier for us to do. Emotional hurt is something we have all experienced, not because it was meant to be that way but rather because our society teaches us certain rules and regulations of behavior. If we feel someone very close to us has broken these rules and regulations, it is a disfavor to us; and our world, our emotional self, tends to crumble. At these times we go further into a state of losing that love, that wonderful love, which tells us You Are Love. We may find ourselves being depressed over a matter. We may hurt or blame someone for our misfortune, or worst still, we may blame ourselves.

If we were to calmly, peacefully, and serenely face our life's obstacles as they happen and consider each of them to be equal, it would not be hard to maintain that love we were born with. The child that was born in our bodies tends to cry out to us in these instances yet we are not in a place to hear these cries for what we term the difficulty of the moment is what haunts our minds and allows our bodies to react in a negative way. There is a growing cumulative effect going on which, of course, none of us is aware of. By the age of five or six we have already burdened ourselves with unwanted baggage. In some small way by that age we know what it is to suffer. It might have been just an incident with a parent, a disagreement with a sibling, a course problem with a teacher, or a little dispute with a friend.

By the time one reaches adulthood, the load of negativity is very heavy for us. It is this immensity which further aggravates the real love, the true love, of which every human is made up of. We are all overburdened by the time we are adults. We use the word love but it has in total certainty lost its trueness.

The problems of day to day living are overwhelming to us. Everything, or nearly everything, becomes a big deal. There are no little things that bother us! Everything is gigantic in scope! We feel that we must act upon everything and make it right. By so doing, there is a significant chance we only make matters worse and the love we knew as the innocent children has dissipated. We listen to others for help and assistance but they, too, are living with this strain. It really doesn't matter what they may tell you. You find yourself saying, "that's not working for me." It's not working because you and you alone need to find the way back. You can regain the love, the true love that you were born with. It is the love that strongly suggests, You Are Love. We are all children of the Divine! We are all products of what our beloved Archangel Raphael referred to as the Age of Innocence.

Before we began our journey on this earthly planet, God gave each of us the love that was so tenderly exemplified during the Age of Innocence. We will cover this in a later chapter. God's love permeated our very Being even as we came out of a womb of someone unknown to us at the time. It deeply touched our soul as well. In line with these facts, our Divine God made it possible for us to become one with all those already on Earth. And, when union of this sort is a fact, then experiences present themselves as only Joy. We were totally and completely filled with the truest love possible by our Divine God, and if we feel there is something missing in our lives, it may be regained, for our Divine God wants only the very best for us. We must in earnest believe this!

— 3 —

OUR SOULS ARE ONE
WITH THE DIVINE GOD

The soul lives on forever and incarnates from one lifetime to another. The soul is created by our Divine God. His love is breathed into it. It is meant for God's love to always remain in the soul, but at times this is not the case.

Some believe the soul is that part that consists of one's thoughts and personality. We all have souls no matter if we are humans or belong to the animal kingdom. The word soul often is discussed by many religions. It is the essence of life and death and rebirth.

Plato thought the soul to be that which determines the manner in which we behave. He considered this essence as an intangible, eternal inhabitant of ourselves. Aristotle, on the other hand, defined the soul as the core of a human being but did not believe it had its own existence.

The Muslim philosopher, Avicenna's view of the soul was that the immortality of it was a direct outcome of its nature. He did not believe it had a purpose to fulfill.

Thomas Aquinas understood the soul to be the first code of the body. His epistemological theory necessitated that since the soul is responsive in recognizing and acknowledging all material things, the soul was not corporeal. He believed the soul had a function which was separate from the body and could exist without the body.

In the Buddhist tradition, the analysis is that there are three minds. The very subtle mind which isn't disintegrated in incarnation-death; the subtle mind which is disintegrated in death and the gross mind. The gross mind doesn't exist when a person is asleep and that makes it impermanent, even more than the subtle-mind, which doesn't exist in death. The very subtle mind tends to catch on to phenomena again, and thus emerges a new subtle mind with its own set of habits and personality.

The Sanskrit words in Hindu which most closely relate to the soul are "Jiva/Atma," which mean individual soul or personality of soul, and "Atman", which also refers to the soul. God is the Supreme Soul. There are many versions in Hinduism of the soul as there are in the other religions presented here.

In Islam, reference is made to the verses from Qur'an. The following information may be extrapolated. In part 15 verse 29, the creation of a human involves Allah breathing a soul into the human. If a person leads a righteous life, the individual will share a nearness to God. In the afterlife, an individual's soul enjoys a time of peacefulness and happiness. Some refer to this as a spiritual growth process until judgment day when both the body and soul are reunited. It is at this juncture the person is rewarded with heaven if they followed God's teachings, or punished if they disobeyed God. This may be found in Qur'an 66:8, 29:20.

In Jainism, the soul, or Jiva as it is referred to, exists as an authenticity. It has a separate subsistence from the body that is its 'umbrella'. The Jiva is different from the non-soul or non-living reality, which consists of time, space, and matter. For those who follow Jainism, the acceptance of the soul and its deliverance are the highest objectives to strive for.

Jewish beliefs of the soul go back to the book of Genesis, verse 2:7 which says, "Hashem formed man from the dust of the earth. He blew into his nostrils the breath of life and man became a living being." Maimonides, in his work "The Guide to the Perplexed," thought of the soul as an individual's intellect without any substance. Gaon, in his discourse on the soul, "Emunoth ve-Deoth 6:3", held the belief that the soul was that part of an individual's mind which dealt with emotions, thought, and physical desires.

In the ancient Israel tradition is the statement, "Then shall the dust return to the earth as it was: and the spirit shall return unto God who gave it" (Ecclesiastes 12:7). Also, in the Corinthians 15:45 "…The first man Adam was made a living soul; the last Adam was made a quickening spirit."

In Kabbalah, the soul is recognized to have three parts. The Zohar, a masterpiece of Jewish beliefs, describes the first as Nephesh. This belief attests to the living being as feeling things such as hate, love, and other emotions, along with death, where one ceases to breath. The second Ruach, is considered to be the middle soul, It has the ability to discern good from evil. The third is Neshama, or the higher soul, sometimes referred to as Higher Self. This higher soul distinguishes one human from all others.

It allows for the belief in an afterlife; it offers one to have the awareness of the presence of God.

Sikism offers that the soul or atma as it is referred to, is a part of the Universal Soul, or God. They often express the belief, "God is in the soul and the soul is in the God," or "The soul is the Lord, and the Lord is the soul,." or "The soul is divine; divine is the soul. Worship him with love." These statements may be found in the holy book, "Sri Guru Granth Sahib".

Augustine, an early Christian, thought of the soul as something endowed with reason. In the Roman Catholic practice, the soul is defined as the innermost aspect of humans. The soul signifies the spiritual aspect. The soul either goes to heaven or hell, based on one's life and dedication to the beauty of it.

Protestants have varied views of the soul but generally believe in the soul's existence.

Mormons feel the soul is a union with the spirit which was previously created by God and later formed by physical conception.

Christadelphians believe we were created from dust and the soul began to exist once the breath of life was received. This was based on the Genesis 2 assumption of creation of person. They also believe once we pass, our breath leaves the body. They believe Christ will return to this earth and those faithful will be given immortality.

In Surat Shabda Yoga, the soul is exactly like the Divine. In Surat Shabda Yoga, it is important to realize one's True Self as soul, True Essence as Spirit Realization and True Divinity as God Realization while conducting life in the physical body. G. I. Gurdjieff thought nobody is ever born with a soul. The soul comes to you due to the manner in which you conduct your life.

As you can see from the above, there are many views on the soul. Some of them are variations of the others, but they are all important and all worthy to note and ponder upon. For our purposes, only very weak sketches were given of the various thoughts on the soul because we want to present what the soul means to Raphael and his teachings.

Our beloved Archangel Raphael believes the soul is the most beautiful entity filled with pure love and given to us by God as the greatest gift ever given to any human being. The body will fracture. It may turn old in time! It will decay when put into the ground after we die, but the soul lives forever. It lives from one lifetime to another. A soul may take a very short time between incarnations or a very long time. It is up to the soul to decide. At times, the Angels will consult in all their loving glory as to when a soul wants to return to the Universe.

All those in the celestial realms want to see the soul's return to earth for they feel it is on this earth and interactions with others that a great deal may be accomplished for others and for our Divine God. It is always time for new developments to occur and for innovative tasks to be performed. Our celestial realm is interested in standing by and just watching and looking to see what each soul has accomplished in a lifetime on this earth of ours This is merely an observation; there are certainly no castigatory actions involved when a soul is unable to accomplish very much.

Every soul writes up a plan while in heaven between lifetimes of what they'd like to accomplish in their next incarnation. Our Divine God makes it quite clear there is no place like "hell". When a soul comes home, it is greeted with the utmost love and respect.

No punitive actions are ever a part of the equation. The celestial realms including our Divine God consider life to be too precious. Each soul when it returns home is greeted harmoniously in a manner of holiness pre-planned by our Divine God.

The Angels go out of their way to show love to the soul returning home, for the journey on our earthly planet in the current now is not an easy one, although it is changing. Each soul should be proud of what they have accomplished on this earth when they live to be only seven years old or a ripe old age of ninety-eight or older. For a soul's coming to this earth is a magnificent thing. It is something which cannot be explained easily for the soul is so very complex. Even those actions which are performed and considered pessimistic by some on the earthly planes are considered to be dear as learning comes from them. Archangel Raphael refers to the soul as a jewel of light and many fantastic colors representing the love of our world and the celestial realms.

It is known through history of the many strong men and women who have walked this earth of ours, accomplished much and returned home, either to wait for the right time to come back, plan a spectacular comeback knowing the world needs it or just taking a rest from a time on our earthly planet. But, it is not just such 'well known' personalities that we are referring to. It is every human being who comes to earth, who may live in a small insignificant town, or a big city, or in a continent not very inhabited and the like.

Basically, it was something the soul wanted to do and every soul has accomplished something. We want to emphasize this dramatically because so many people nowadays feel like, "what am I doing here? My life is such a mess! I'm not getting anything done." These statements flow like water over geese every minute of every day. Yet, these are human statements which in the end don't have too much relevance. In fact, they may be referred to as useless statements when each and every human realizes they are love.

After we pass and our soul reaches heaven, there are many Angels to greet us. These Angels show us a great deal of love, affection, and respect. The treatment is the same for all souls. There are no class systems in heaven. We were all created by God and that's the way it will always be. We are on the same level as those in the celestial realms as they, too, were created by God. We may consider ourselves all a part of our Divine God because of his creation of us.

The Angels, whose mission is to work for God and humanity, want to assist us in the afterlife as much as they can. In our own manner and theirs, we are able to discuss our experiences on earth. We can look at the original plan we made up before leaving heaven for earth and see how it lines up with what we have accomplished. We can confide in all of God's helpers with how we feel about having been on this earth during this incarnation. Some of us may want to come back right away. This is possible after a new plan is drawn up. We may put in the new plan exactly what we'd like to do, how long we'd like to be here, whether or not we want to marry, who we'd like to be born to, how we'd like to help others and everything else that is pertinent to our life on this earth.

Those on the celestial realms never push nor do they punish a soul about anything! Their only duty is to help and love. This can only be emphasized over and over again. At times when a soul finds difficulty in assessing whether or not to come back to earth, our Divine God assists that soul in the decision-making process but ultimately the soul decides. Karma in a very natural way does come up and unless it is somehow eradicated it will be troublesome to the soul in the next lifetime or several lifetimes to come. Our Divine God is able to recognize Karma immediately in a soul and sometimes it may be eradicated in heaven through a special connection with either Archangel Raphael or others in the celestial realms. Other times, it is necessary to fulfill the needs of Karma through some splendid actions on this Earth in one's next lifetime before a soul can be completely cleansed of it.

Our beloved Archangel Raphael feels that the soul, just like the physical self, is made up of love, pure love, from our Divine God. Before going on any further, it seems appropriate to give just a very short biographical sketch on Archangel Raphael for those who may not know much about this startling Archangel. Raphael, whose name in Hebrew means, "God Has Healed." He is one of the most beloved Archangels of all time. His name happened because Raphael was credited with healing our Earth of diseases when it was defiled by the sons of fallen angels as told in the Apocryphal Book of Enoch.

Raphael is one of the seven archangels who stand before the Lord, referred to in Tobit 12:15 and in Revelation 8:2. He is referred to as the angelic healer and is associated with the throat chakra. His special duty has been protecting the young, the innocent, and the traveler. Raphael is the archangel of love, healing, light, and science. Archangel Raphael is known for his magnificent energy healings and his belief that love and loving ways may be successfully utilized to handle life's day-to-day situations.

Archangel Raphael emphatically believes the soul is love. It is total, pure love.

Why? Because each and every soul is created by our Divine God and since God is pure love, so is each and every soul that God creates.

The soul of an infant just removed from the womb of a woman is one hundred percent love. The first cry that child gives is love. And, of course, the physical self of that infant is true and pure love. From the first day on this earth, the soul of every human being is challenged by those who have been here longer than the time when that infant appeared on this earth.

Everything is a test to the infant because of the manner in which our society operates. There are the very early years from infancy to about five years old when the child relies upon those he or she is living with whether it be parents, a single mother, single father, foster parents, or an institution of one sort or another. The child tends to take on the words and even actions of those that are in charge. In some instances, the influences are congruent with the plan the soul has drawn up while still in heaven. In other cases a different story exists. The child is not in harmony with his or her plan and it has a strong negative effect on the soul not to mention the child's physical self.

At that young and early age the child accepts whatever words or actions come their way, be they gracious or harmful. This already puts a massive burden on the child and what it is to follow. Many expressions and actions of our guardians are loving and positive but there are those that are doubtful in nature. It is safe to assume that by age five a child already has been a sufferer of some word or action that would alter the pure love of the soul and physical self.

As the child grows older, this phenomenon continues, and in most cases, the child who has been the victim of certain actions will inflict those words or actions on a sibling or peer, parent or teacher. And, this does go on, which always tends to diminish the love that was the pure love of the soul.

In adulthood this phenomenon becomes even stronger. We find ourselves in conflicting situations which we handle badly. Our lives become full of frustration. There are so many problems! No one cares for me! No one really loves me! Oh, sure, my husband says he loves me, but he's out there having an affair with a co-worker. The woman next door says she's my friend but tells everyone she comes into contact with terrible stories about me which aren't true. I lost faith in my religious beliefs, and I feel there shouldn't be such a thing as religion anyhow. One could go on and on, for the challenges that we are presented with never seem to disappear.

The pure love of the soul which God gave us seems to have dissipated. Where has it gone? And, most of all can it be regained? Our plan for this earth is completely forgotten for if it were remembered our words and actions of our physical self would coincide with it automatically. We certainly want our soul to be the love it was, for it is this love which will allow us to help humanity as a whole, enrich our lives, and reach our highest goal, that which is Joy.

All humans have a basic instinct of wanting to help others. Some are bitter and this would certainly distract from allowing us to lend a hand to others. Some feel they are the only important ones in the world and what they have matters. Others have simply lost sight of the fact that they are able to help others. This all comes from the fact that our soul has lost a portion or all of the love it came to earth with.

For with a healthy physical self and soul, the tendency is to help humanity. That comes first on the list of priorities. What we want is miniscule compared to that! By being a part of the celestial realm and a distinct, beautiful part of our Divine God, this is without reservation what is important to us. All of us may consider ourselves part of the celestial realms, and those in the celestial realms at the current time, i.e. Angels, may consider themselves humans if they wish. This is basic truth because our souls have experienced both. Angels, through their enduring efforts, have also experienced both.

Without even thinking about it, we know it is more important to infuse the soul with love. A cleansed soul is one filled with total and complete pure love. It is ready to give help and assistance to those most in need, and in doing so, our lives are automatically enriched.

— 4 —

THE HAPPINESS OF BEING

God wants us to know unequivocally through the angelic realm, Archangel Raphael, and others that our physical self and soul are love because we are, in fact, part of the great plan. Our physical self must be maintained in the best way we know how. It is most important to keep ourselves healthy, loving, kind, and keepers of the great phenomenon which is life itself. The pure love of the soul needs to be constantly nourished by us

The word "being" means in the stratum of great things, our holy existence on this earth. "Being" also means to so many on a spiritual path, a human self. Being can also beautifully refer to the soul. The greatest meaning of the word "being" is that we are a direct connection to our Divine God on this magnificent haven we refer to as earth.

I remember when I was a little girl of five how active I was. Living in a small town, my friends were mostly my family and neighbors. I was considered a tomboy as I loved doing innocent things like climbing trees, working the garden, playing, and listening to the guidance of my brilliant mother. I thought she knew it all. Everything she ever told me in those early years was taken seriously. I was so happy! I was so unencumbered with unwanted activity. I think my life then was just a bowl of cherries.

I truly believe when I think back on those times that from birth until I went to first grade, I was following my original plan.

When I entered first grade at the age of five everything changed, and I remember questioning why it was so different. My mom would try to explain to me that I was at a different level of life. However, I can honestly say I was never satisfied with that answer. It was not the way it was meant to be. And, throughout my life, I questioned the need for my life to be so different from what I had expected it to be. Working with Angels, I now believe they had given me insights into my life and why changes which I didn't want were happening to me. I honestly believe that from an early age I fought bravely to stay on a course that I outlined for myself and which God verified to me in one way or the other as spectacular.

It was our Divine God's idea to match so beautifully and gracefully our physical body and soul in each of our incarnations. God felt by this wonderful match it would make our life on this earth substantial in carrying out our mission. A mission is chosen by us while still in heaven. We come to earth and truly have great answers which would help the populace, but through our acquaintances, world conditions such as wars, and inhumanities, an individual tends to diminish the greatness of existence.

There is nothing greater than existence. There is nothing greater at any given time than to know that an individual is endowed with a physical body which acts in a manner that in a sense coincides with our soul thinking. For when we are here on earth, the soul certainly isn't a dormant entity. The soul is the basis for our creation and therefore our efforts are on behalf of ourselves, those we love, and all of humanity.

The soul may constantly reach to our Divine God for assistance while on this earth and it will get that which it needs in any current time. Our Divine God in creating us, has given us the talent which is the same as the Divine's talent and thereby making our tasks less tedious and more rewarding.

He asks of us one thing and that is that we allow the love in our physical self and soul to overflow throughout the earth mingling with as many others as possible for the common good of all humans. There is something to the belief that the soul is a direct extension of us to the heavens. It is like a blissful pathway directly to our Divine God which is open at all times, day or night, Monday or Sunday. It doesn't matter. This direct pathway allows us to have contact with the celestial realms at any given time. So, in a logistical approach, the soul connects with the Divine Master whenever there is a need for it to do so.

The physical self and soul are directly connected as well. The soul in a sense guides the physical self through life due to the plan that was drawn up by the soul. Many times the physical self tends to ignore the reasoning of the soul and does that which it feels is best. In doing so, it may hurt itself in the process, as the physical self is very sensitive to the ways of the world and becomes frustrated, angered, non-committal, unable to make wise decisions, disrespectful of other humans and the like.

If we follow the adage, "all humans have something beautiful to offer," it will help us in dealing with them. There are so many instances that the physical self blunders rather than follow acceptance. The soul only knows positivity, and this is passed on from the soul to the physical self. There are so many times we don't hear the message of the soul because of the composite of our birth, education, and work life. We tend to be stubborn about matters.

We must remember always the soul gives the physical self messages which are directly from the Divine God. He wants only the best for us. He wants us to have an enriched life. God wants us to succeed in helping humanity. He wants us all to experience Joy. He is not unhappy with us if we return home without that experience but he is a lot happier and rejoices with us if we do have that experience. Our Divine God wants us to enjoy the ultimate in each incarnation.

Being is a lovely state we are in when coming to this earth and following our plan and overcoming obstacles. In our being we have the opportunity to fill another's life with splendor and it is becoming to do so each and every day of our existence from the time we know what that means. Our interactions with others are of a being nature. Our plan for life is of this nature.

Suppose you were twenty-three years old, a college graduate, with a fairly good job. Each and every night you thought about your own good time and how you might acquire this good time. You don't care if you use a person and then drop him/her off by the wayside because you're done with them. Or, when you see the individual the next time you hardly speak because the person is not your type. Or, because you know that person only likes good times, you constantly ask that person to join you in a night of eating, drinking, smoking, dancing and carousing. You get home at four in the morning and you're up at eight to get to your job for nine. You tell everyone what a wonderful time you had, time and time again. Others may think, "How can she or he keep doing that and not get tired?" or, "Isn't she or he interested in anything but a good time?, or "She's wonderful; or he's wonderful, I wish I could do that."

This goes on for many years! Suddenly, you have this huge awakening. It is actually your soul messaging your body that the life you are living is not healthy. You might become seriously ill if you continue with it in that manner.

You are far from following the plan that put you on this earth. You are not accomplishing anything spiritual, loving, or helpful. It is all about you and the fun you want to have for yourself. What you don't realize was that your soul was giving you that message all along. You just didn't want to hear it. This might have been due to the people you worked with, your early upbringing and those who looked after you, teachers in school, or even those around you which were your friends and acquaintances. We in no way want to express the notion that the life and actions described above are wrong, for our Divine God believes that nothing is wrong. It is only mistaken if it hurts others or yourself. In this case, a fast life may conceivably hurt you.

The awakening can take place at any time in one's life, and then it is possible to follow a plan of love, a righteous life filled with giving to others; those who you may know and those you may not know.

It is never too late for the awakening and the soul never gives up to let the physical self know whether they are on the path or not.

Being is a pleasant state when we offer another human being something which allows them to become a better person. Those who were here many years ago, left to go to heavenly realms and returned, know the feeling. To offer another person something is an unexplainable act of great fortune. Even the littlest of things mean a great deal. Sometimes it is exactly what your friend, neighbor, family member, co-worker needs to get himself/herself back on a spiritual track of the highest nature. If we allow it to happen, flowing thoughts of love embrace us and these sacred thoughts reach our hearts and help us on the trail of our plan. They will also touch those we are willing to share our love with, for the Divine God's love was meant to be shared in a great way. All matter, whether it is human, animal, or vegetable, will benefit from this process of love we are willing to offer others.

If you see a little animal, such as a cat or dog, it is so nice to take a moment to pet the animal and whisper something beautiful and unusually loving to the cat or dog. If we see a bird perched on the window sill, reach out with love to that bird and tell it in plain English that you love it. It is this type of concern for others, humans or animal, which will not only allow them to act and spread the goodness in their kingdom, whatever it may be, but will allow you to spread the love that you are made of. The more love you can spread the better chance the world has of becoming one of total love.

Wouldn't you like to see a world filled with love from the air you breathe, to all of human life, animal and bird life, waters, all vegetation and so forth?. It was this way thousands of years ago as our beloved Archangel Raphael tells us about it. He was here on earth and has seen it and has lived it.

One point to remember that might be underscored is the fact that once the process begins, it has a stunning visual effect. We, as humans, will recognize the change and it will encourage us to carry out our plan with a zest and vitality like the world has not seen. It will be a fantastic time to rejoice, for efforts will be realized. The year 2012 is one in which most humans will recognize an aggregate amount of positive change. They will know the work they have done up to that time was not in vain but rather it was the seeds planted by everyone who followed their plan to make the world a place in which lives become enriched, important discoveries made, health issues and diseases lessened, and where spiritual life will be the pathway to Joy. .

Being may also be a state of calmness. By this we mean being is a time to reflect with our Divine Creator and just enjoy the moment. As spirituality becomes dominant in the world, so does meditation. Do you remember a time when you were in your total being in such a magnificent way that you can honestly say you never felt like that before?

You were without a doubt being in a state of calmness. You were united with our Divine God. It was a time when you wanted this to happen more than anything else and it happened. It is in these moments of complete calmness a person draws a masterpiece for the beauty of the world. It may be a flower such as a rose and that flower carries the love that you have within. It may bloom and then wither as flowers do but the love from that flower somehow permeates the air and spreads to other roses and so the love flows and lovingly lives on.

Being is considered to be a state of greatness. This is not a conceited greatness. It is a pure loving greatness that all humans have. It has been stressed before and it's important to say again, the greatness of an individual is the same as the greatness of our Divine Master, our God. This greatness allows our lives to have a meaning far beyond our expectations. The greatness of our world is so encompassing it allows for its magnitude to engulf us with love. Realization and usage may provide all we were meant to have.

It is in the moments of sadness, depression, loneliness, anger, hatred, and other such negative attributes that we prevent our growth in terms of the loving beauty we have to offer for this world to become a most loving place. When any of the above mentioned and others try to capture you, find your spot of calmness and retreat to it, for it is the healer which will allow you to move forward like a spiritual soldier.

Our Divine God, Ascended Masters, Archangels, Angels, and others in the angelic realms want us to be happy and productive. They were all here so they know exactly how our world operates. Being God's helpers for humanity, they will help us get through any difficulties we encounter. They know the world is a difficult place especially if one's plan cannot be followed. But, they also know that each soul left heaven for earth with a most striking plan to make it a better place and to help humanity. It is also well to note here if we haven't previously, that the plan of each soul is slightly different, just as each soul in itself is different from another soul. No two physical bodies are exactly the same, either. This is God's way of saying that we are all beautiful creatures of the earth and should think of ourselves in that manner, without conceit.

Each time a soul incarnates, the soul decides whether it wants to be male or female. Each incarnation is deemed sacred by our Divine God and the soul who finds a physical body.

Sometimes the question arises whether or not the physical self and soul may terminate a plan before it was meant to be that way. The answer is yes. There is nothing written in concrete! There may be a time a soul comes to earth, forms a physical body and proceeds on their plan. That individual may find it was not the right time to be here and thus the soul wants to leave the body and return to heaven. The Divine God grants such petitions and is understanding of them. However, this does not happen often. Maybe one in several millions or so! Generally, the physical self faces the challenges squarely and wants to succeed at what it is he/she is to achieve.

Being is a state of truth in how we convey a thought or message to another individual. This is an important aspect as on our earth what is discouraging to us at times is that we don't hear the truth and we, ourselves, don't relay the truth to others. If an individual meditates on it, the truth appears.

When you were in school and the teacher asked a question, oftentimes the answer given was one to please the teacher, not yourself. Sometimes, your given policy was not to question just respond in accord with societal beliefs. And, you did this with your friends, too, and they back to you. It seems no one wants to hurt the others feelings. When you began dating and a boy wanted sex and you didn't, you may have been afraid to say no. It's not the right time for me! I want to wait until marriage or you're not the one I want to have sex with. Truth may not have been reiterated. What followed was sorrow and hurt and a feeling of degradation. This might have continued in your adult life. I can't tell him/her what I really think. I'll just say something that will please them. Never mind me!

There are many disagreements between individuals

because of this behavior, but no one wants to take responsibility. They rather continue masking the truth. In a work situation, it is true that you need to follow the directions of your boss, but you need never be talked down to or abused or forced into something you don't want to do. You need to express what it is you expect. In many instances you are looking for respect as all humans do. No human deserves less! It is always important to make it known, through various different means, that respect is expected, and by the same token, respect is given.

After marriage and children, there may have been arguments over money. You say whatever you need to in order to pacify your mate. When it comes to the children, it seems you need to agree for the truth would cause severe arguments and possibly other undesirable repercussions. A plan made in the celestial realms is falling apart.

Being is a state of truth so an individual may never be wrong or go wrong by stating his/her true beliefs in any situations. There are many sides to a story, and hopefully the best one will be chosen for a loving, harmonious life. When there is acute pressure on an individual to constantly be agreeable because they are afraid to tell it like is, this is very bad for one's emotional well-being. It causes the ripple effect that just goes on and on to the next incident that occurs and then the next and so forth.

Our Divine God wants us to know there is a direct passageway from our human being to the Divine God and that path is one of truth. It is only in truth that progress may be attained in making the world a better place for humankind, which we all want to see happen. It will enrich our lives as well. The dreadful ripple effect of falsehood will become eradicated.

To be truthful, an individual doesn't need to be vicious

or use foul language. One may be very loving and still be truthful. This is how we become accustomed to using our words, for there are enough words in every language throughout the world that express all ideas and thoughts in loving ways. We don't need to jeopardize our relationships with our spouse, family, friends, co-workers, boss, and others. What is needed is a loving approach!

This loving approach is extended to our actions, too, for words and the way we say them have meaning. Our physical self has a way of appearing when we are angry, for example, and a different way of looking when there is love. Now which is better? This doesn't take much thought to realize that it is a beautiful happening when one synchronizes body and words in a loving manner. It is without a doubt a blessing for the individual you are speaking with to witness it. .How do you think they will answer you?

It will be with love, for love creates more love.

When one is truthful, deeds become so much more meaningful. One individual gives something to another with love. When deeds are performed because "I have to do this," there is a recognizable element to them for the person on the receiving end. Though the person receiving the deed may say, "thank you," they will not forget the origin of the deed. It was not done from love for one person to another person. It was simply an artificial act and carries a zero on a scale of one to ten.

The person receiving it sees it written in bold letters of distrust because it is done many times as an afterthought. Other times it is simply done to pacify or quiet the other person from thinking the worst. Still other times the sadness and unhappiness the other person feels by such acts only further detract from love. It is not a direction showing someone that a caring, loving attitude prevails.

The benefits of such misdirected actions are less than minimal and the experience of them is less than meaningful in a series of events. In a broader sense, doing something for someone because you feel you have to distracts from your being and your love for all of humanity, and the same is true for the receiver. For in the world where it's important to look at the broader picture and act accordingly with love if we are to impact the true nature of being and why it is we are here, less than that is considered to be inappropriate, inadequate and unacceptable.

Our love for ourselves, our loved ones, those around us and all of humanity is based on unselfish deeds. Most of us want to show love to all, for it is in this way that we will build a world which rings forward in a loving way. Our own lives will be enriched; the lives of those in our households, on the streets, in the cities, countries, continents will be enriched. One small action from an individual carries with it the possibility of influencing the world as a whole. It is certain that is what each of us wanted as we were in the heavens awaiting a new birth for ourselves. We watched and were able to see justification for it in this age more so than those past except for the glorious times of thousands of years ago. We were there in the heavens thinking thoughts which only our souls know for the deepness of the soul carries them.

Many souls coming to earth in this current now are ready for the year 2012 and the high expectations of an amazing life those living will have. There will no doubt be a flooding of souls coming to earth for this rebirth of the world in 2012, as they want to be here to take part in the most valuable happenings the time will offer.

The expectations in the celestial realms are soaring for the new era and beyond. Our Divine Creator, God, wants humankind to relish an existence of purity, love, enhancement, knowledge, enrichment and the like. They, in the heavens, including those souls who have departed from our earth, are there waiting and wondering whether a return to earth in the new era will be a time that they can accomplish much for humanity. Will the reward for living in the new era be the beginning of a threshold so magnificent that only our Divine God can fully describe it? Celestial beings and souls who were once here think beyond the ordinary that we were thought to think.

It is important to ponder now as we walk the trail of life with our spiritual givings in total control. For it is true that even our thoughts may create that which we most want.

Being is seeing the Light of God and becoming and staying a part of God for the duration of existence on this earthly planet. It is such a superb feeling to know that God's pure love directs one to see beyond the normal. When we speak of seeing, we don't mean looking out the window and watching the snow fall. We don't mean seeing a neighbor next door. We don't mean seeing what's on the shelves of a grocery store.

The seeing that we are talking about is always seeing our Divine Creator, our God, and being one with him. This seeing is indelibly in our physical self and soul. No matter what happens it will not ever become lost or less functional. From the time we appear on this earth this great Light of Lights, this seeing, is within ourselves. Many of us don't know we have this gift from God. Some of us may go through our entire lives without any knowledge of it. Those who know find their lives are more focused, cherished, loving, giving, and enriched.

When I was just a young girl of nine, I constantly had a vision of an airplane going down close to where we lived. We lived near an Air Force base and there was always a lot of activity overhead. I must admit the loud sound of low flying planes always bothered me at that age. If I was out of doors, I tried to hurry inside my home or some other building. At first I kept this to myself but then told my mother about what I felt. She hugged me and told me not to worry because nothing would happen to me. One day, as I was out of doors playing with a neighbor girl, we heard this tremendously loud thud-like noise and it came from the direction of the airport. My friend and I ran into the house and I asked my mother if she heard it. She said yes. Later we found out an airplane was in trouble landing and strayed off the landing strip. No one was hurt. It was an upsetting happening, and the whole town talked about it for weeks.

About two years ago, my sister-in-law, who lived next door to me, called me. She was very excited. I was interested in learning why. It seems that night she was in bed, the curtains pulled, when all of a sudden she saw this light in the room. It had illuminated the entire room. Then she saw a figure of a beautiful woman dressed in white and blue. The woman just looked at her lovingly. My sister-in-law became frightened and didn't say anything to her. When she told me this story, it immediately came to me that she had a visit from Mother Mary. I told my sister-in-law how happy I was for her, for a visit from Mother Mary is no small matter. I reiterated how blessed she should feel.

I thought about it after we hung up, and it came to

me from our Divine God that my sister-in-law is ready to make the journey home and soon would no longer be with us.

Two weeks later, my sister-in-law died.

Those who never find God's wisdom speaking to them every minute of every day are sealed to the knowledge of this seeing. This becomes a massive detriment to their judgment, thinking, acting, and the love they are able to give themselves, their close ones and humanity as All. In this awareness of seeing, the soul and body are balanced in love for anything God does is love. The soul becomes nourished and becomes a greater entity for accepting God's love. It is the presence of this seeing that love is carried to its most spectacular extremes.

Seeing plays an important role in how our lives unfold. Our Divine God guides us through this window of love so that we would not depart from our original plan. Seeing is a process which may not come quickly for some. It may require certain individuals to do either relaxation or meditation exercises because the eye of seeing as we speak of it here runs through our entire body and soul with a connection to our Divine God.

To gain insights that are truly out of the ordinary in being but necessary to our life's joy, an entity such as we are must visualize intently that which is to be achieved. Once a formula appears to work for an individual, it becomes natural to have this connection with God and receive answers to any questions which may arise. As we mentioned previously, questions should be considered just that; they are neither small or large; good or bad. They just are.

There are those who adhere to the premise that this type of visualization is beyond the ordinary. Being guided by the eye of the Divine God within us allows us the conscious opportunity to gain the knowledge necessary in understanding even the most problematic issues. We will see them not as difficult but rather as routine in carrying out our loving role on this earth for ourselves, and all of humanity.

Being is but a most amazing aspect of human existence.

— 5 —

THE DIVINE GOD
MESHES IN OUR HEARTS

Ask anyone what they think about first when the word heart is mentioned. Many will tell you the heart signifies a feeling of love and affection one person has for another. When one becomes engaged, they tell each other, "I love you with all my heart." Later, when they are married and Valentine's Day rolls around the husband will buy his wife a box of chocolates shaped like a heart to designate his love.

After a quibble or fight, one spouse may tell the other, "I love you, but I just can't agree with what you're saying." If one breaks off a relationship, one may say, "I love you very much but I can't marry you. It's not the right time for me."

In a time of divorce, one or the other may express the heaviness and emptiness they feel in their heart. How can they go on in life without their partner who was so close to their heart day in and day out. What happened to the love of the heart?

A mother may become angry at the antics of her loved ones, yet her heart goes out to them in times of trouble. If a sibling is ill, another sibling will feel that pain in their heart and express some sort of affection so that their brother or sister will get well.

Many people will say, "My heart can't stand it!" What they really want to say is their entire physical being needs a change.

When we like something that we are given or told, we might say, "Bless your heart." What a beautiful, heartwarming answer.

The heart is a powerful organ of our bodies. If we listen to our heart a great deal of goodness may be accomplished. Our heart is the organ of the physical self which most clearly resembles the soul even though the heart stops one day and the individual dies, whereas the soul lives on and on forever. Some thinkers believe the heart is the place where life begins and ends. When one is discharged from the womb and slapped on the butt by a doctor, it begins the life cycle. The heart at that point begins to pump. As previously mentioned, when we take our last breath, the heart stops, and life stops. The soul advances to the heavens.

The heart is oftentimes a symbol in many religions and beliefs. Our medical people believe that the great amount of authority of the heart is really located in the brain. Our upbringing, however, points to the fact that the heart is residence for all of our emotions.

The great comedienne, Martha Raye, always ended her musical variety shows on television with "Good night, Sisters." She thanked the nuns at The Sisters of St. Francis

Hospital in Miami, Florida where she recovered from health problems. Well wishers at the hospital gave her a St. Christopher's medal, a St. Genesius medal and a Star of David which she faithfully wore. She was a famous star yet never forgot those who helped her, and they had shared a oneness. It touched one's heart.

Vivien Leigh, the extremely talented British actress who won the title role in "Gone With the Wind," did a spectacular job as Scarlett O'Hara. Those who saw the movie will never forget the famous line she spoke, "I'll never be hungry again!" She did the role and particularly this line with such dramatic supremacy that it not only touched one's heart, it made an individual think about all those hungry people all over the world. What oneness!

Milton Berle, Uncle Miltie as he was affectionately called, another great comic of that era, used the song, "Near Me," as his theme song. It melted one's heart to hear the orchestra play the song and Mr. Berle come out and do his act. One sensed the capacity for love he had for all people. His audience inevitably became one.

Mary Martin was a Broadway musical actress, whose fame was worldwide and her successes many, particularly her role as Nellie Forbush in South Pacific. Every song she ever sang was done in a manner which was strictly Martin. One would say she had two voices; one which she used for one type of song, another for a different category of song. Her talent was extraordinary and it touched everyone's heart.

Will Rogers, the classic Cherokee-American cowboy, movie star, and humorist, was known as Oklahoma's favorite son. He made some 50 silent films and 21 talkies. Will Rogers wrote over 4,000 syndicated newspaper columns. He became known and adored all over the world.

His voice was of a certain type and became familiar with audiences. He played himself in many films, didn't put on the normal makeup, ad-libbed a lot and his commentaries on politics were widely listened to. He is remembered for all of these feats but perhaps most was his famous line, "I never yet met a man that I didn't like." The emphasis was on "yet" and this became a signature quote in many of his public performances. It made everyone's heart sing to see and listen to Will Rogers and when he uttered the above words, it was as if a Light from heaven came down to the audience and the warmth touched everyone's heart.

Ethel Merman, another great of the New York stage, belted out a song like no other person could. The theater's seats and floors would virtually shake when she sung. Your heart skipped a few beats when listening to this enormous talent.

Lucille Ball, the great American comedienne, film and stage actress, film executive and star of the landmark sitcom "I Love Lucy" perhaps enjoyed one of the longest careers of Hollywood's stars. She won four Emmy Awards, the Golden Globe, the Lifetime Achievement Award and the Academy of Television Arts & Sciences Governors Award. When I Love Lucy came on TV people hightailed it back home from wherever they were just to see her show. There was something not only funny about this great woman, but also she brought a spirituality to one's heart. Everyone loved Lucy.

Elvis Presley was known all over the world simply as Elvis. Some referred to him as the King of Rock and Roll or just The King. He was born in a two-room house in Tupelo, Mississippi. His voice was such that he not only sang rock and roll but did gospel, blues, ballads and pop. He performed across the United States but mostly in

Las Vegas. His concerts were booked months in advance. Wherever he appeared the crowds mounted to get a glimpse or listen to him sing. He brought joy to the hearts of so many.

Jackie Gleason was a fantastic comedic talent, a musician in his own right, and an actor. His great talent was found in his development of such characters as Joe the Bartender, The Poor Soul, Reginald Van Gleason III., Loudmouth Charlie Bratton, to mention only a few. Jackie Gleason will always be remembered for the role of Ralph Kramden in The Honeymooners. In his variety show, Jackie always found a spot to reiterate, "How sweet it is!" What lovely words that made one feel good and lifted one's heart with happiness.

Farrah Fawcett born in Texas as Mary Farrah Leni Fawcett, will always be remembered for her role as one of the Angels in Charlie's Angels. Some say she was the girl next door. Fawcett was beautiful and her fantastic hair style was loved by millions. Hairdressers all over the world scrambled to beautician's workshops to learn how to do a Farrah Fawcett haircut, including my sister, Fran.

Through her approval of a documentary detailing the steps of the cancer she suffered, she showed the world that suffering can be changed to love. Everyone will remember this enormous gift of love she gave humankind. How beautiful! Farrah Fawcett, an actress, a mother, but most of all an Angel, forever.

Frederick Chopin, the famous composer, was born in Poland, but he lived most of his adult life in France. Before he died at a very early age, he requested in his will that his heart be sent to Poland for burial. His heart was removed and preserved in alcohol. His sister, Ludwika Jedrzejewicz, took it to Warsaw in an urn, where it was preserved within the Holy Cross Church in a pillar. There was an inscription from Matthew VI:21:"For where your treasure is, there will your heart be also." Chopin's heart was placed near this beautiful and fitting caption. He loved, Poland, his homeland.

There is a huge statue of Chopin in Warsaw's Royal Baths Park. It is said that in tribute to this great pianist, touching Chopin concerts are offered almost weekly. Those who have visited Poland say being there, listening to Chopin music, left their heart feeling renewed and refreshed. What was it in this case? The fact that Chopin, as a musician, was famous. Was it because his music is so stunning? Or, was it because his heart is buried in Poland? Most will say, it's because his heart is buried there. Some believe the heart has a way of silently speaking even after death! In Chopin's case, many believe his music reflected his love for his homeland and all of humanity. His love for humankind gave us no better opportunity than to enhance our love that is in our hearts for one another, whether or not we know them.

The brief sketches given above are, of course, of those most of us can relate to because we either saw them on TV, movies, or in concert. That is why those examples were used. We are all 'well-known' and equal in the Divine God's assessment. The folks mentioned above are no better than any of us. We all have hearts that open up and give so much to others. To realize this is to take a step forward in your spiritual path, thinking, and acting. Your heart as everyone's else's heart is love.

When our pet cat or dog do something cute, like a new trick, it makes us and those around us laugh and be pleased. We praise our little creatures, give them a hug for reaching our hearts.

There are those times, too, when we are specifically asked by someone to do something we don't want to do. We may know the person well. An example would be this. You receive an email which is really uplifting from someone you haven't heard from in a while. It makes your heart feel pretty exhilarated. The individual writing you sounds as if he/she is truly interested in what you are doing in this current now. You can't wait to respond to this pleasant email and update the person on your life situation, especially if things are really going well for you. Okay, so that's what you've done. You've written back. Then you get another email back. This one is less than friendly. It has almost a demanding tone to it as the person you thought to be your friend was only interested in telling you about something they were doing that would cost you money. You do not want to spend your money on it. You immediately notice the difference. Your heart automatically becomes disappointed.

In these kinds of instances it is best to remember not to allow anyone to have power over you. Your heart will tell you clearly when it looks like someone is invading your territory and thus might be changing your dreams, aspirations, loving ways and love for those around you and all of humanity.

Many centuries ago, Galen, a Greek physician experimented with the heartbeat of humans. When whispering the names of loved ones in a person's ear, he found the heartbeat would quicken. The symbol of the heart represents earthly love in the opposite fashion as well. It sometimes becomes 'tight' with envy or jealousy. The heart is used to express so many emotions: courage, grief, devotion, faithfulness, to mention but a few.

In Britain during the 18th century it was a regular

thing to bury the pierced heart of a feral animal to chase away evil spirits.

In ancient Egypt, the populace considered the heart to be the core of our intellect. Romantic love was related to the pulsebeat of the heart. The Egyptians believed the heart had a distinct place in the afterlife. It seemed the heart told them if the person led a 'good' life. The heart was weighed against the symbol of Maat which meant that which is right. There needed to be a balance between the Maat and the heart. If there was no balance, the dead person was eaten up by what they referred to as the devourer which was part lion, hippopotamus and crocodile. Their customs also encouraged that amulets be left with the body so that the heart measurement would be accurate in the evaluation of the departed.

The world renowned artist, Leonardo daVinci, painted the heart with beauty and a tremendous amount of accuracy. He disagreed with Galen on the number of chambers the heart held. He was correct in thinking it was four instead of two. DaVinci was mainly interested in painting the heart accurately rather than representing on canvass the emotions of the heart.

It is often expressed during relaxation or meditation that God and the Center of our heart will become united. As we've mentioned previously, God is an integral part of our physical body as well as our soul because of creation. However, there is a distinctively particular place for uniting with our Divine God and that is deep within our heart region.

Our heart may be compared to the deepest well we can imagine. It goes on and on without ever experiencing an ending. Dare we say our heart can begin at one end of the Universe and finish at another! This is true of all humans, and that is why all we want is to enrich our lives and experience Joy.

It may also be said that the deepest truths of our Universe live in the heart of each human. The answers to all questions, whatever they may be, live in the heart. That is why when someone says, "That's not possible!" everything is possible because of the manner in which our Divine God created us. The deep wells of our hearts are so filled with rapture and love for everyone. It is here we find the love of the ages, our fellow humans, those in the angelic realms and our Divine God. It is from this sacred area that billions of efforts and more are possible.

In the scriptures of the Hindus, a highest truth and the immortal inner self dwells in the heart region. Judaism, Islam and Christianity have similar ideas. In the Old Testament, truth and character of a person is in the heart. Mohammad once said, "When the heart is corrupt, the body is corrupt, and when it is sound, the body is sound." In Christianity, the heart is a focal point for devotion.

"They are not dead who live in our hearts," suggests that the deceased person lives on as long as the memory is in our hearts. In ancient times, and possibly even now, depending on religion and customs, burial of the physical self is separated from burial of the heart. The example of this was given above with Chopin, where at his request his heart went back to Poland. Sometimes, a family member will request this separate burial ceremony because they believe the heart acts as a soul here on Earth.

We all have experiences which are relished and those which are reviled. Some are part of our plan, others are not. Tears show up when we are deeply hurt, or grieving. Our heart, too, sheds tears. It seems an eternity before our heart calms and we don't fester from a catastrophe. When hurt feelings become imbedded in the heart, we and the Divine God understand the many why's of their core. It's in the structure of an individual to hold an emotion in the heart for a long time. There are many times when an individual is unable to share with others what is in their hearts. Some refer to this as "suffering in silence."

When the emotion of hurt encompasses the deepness of your hearts, it may be relieved by letting the tears flow and sharing with loved ones painful emotions. There is an inner sanctuary in our hearts which is very loving and which knows all there is to know in our lives. If we tap into this well of love every time there is a need to do so our lives will become better. We will then be able to escape the pangs of hurt emotions.

Tears may be summarized as one way of achieving a modicum of happiness in this transient world. Even our tears are love, and when wiped away by the beloved hand of the Angels or the Divine God, they go into a beautiful replica container of the heart and are taken to the celestial realms where they are blessed. Tears are a beautiful practice of love.

Tears, too, may oftentimes give us insights into magnetic functions we are to serve on this earth, for we all have the highest capacity to do so. Every human being will intentionally grow from the experience. In a sense this may be related to the nurturing process of the physical self and especially the heart.

This is but one small example of the role hurt may play in our lives and become a positive factor. There are so many pains we allow ourselves to beget. Pain of every kind will go away if we allow it too. Pain brings an individual in the state of holiness, devoutness, and wisdom. Think of a pain suffered and allow that pain to represent something you hated to go through. Now, you think of it as beautiful as it has promoted a growth process within your heart.

The pain an individual suffers directly hits the heart and sometimes happens during the most challenging times of one's life. Maybe we actually needed to go through this as part of our earthly plan to accomplish something later on. If we look at it from the perspective that somewhere down the road of our spiritual life it will bring us a beauty like we've never known before, it will be palatable.

To offset pain, it is best to do something charitable and of benefit to another person. My mother suffered a great deal of pain because my father had cancer and she knew the inevitable was going to happen. He was a young man when stricken. My mother had a large family, and some of the siblings were young. There was the worry of how she would manage. She, herself, had been ill and needed surgery. But, being the amazing woman that she was, she offered people in town whatever she could, be it food items or clothing, a portion of land where they could plant vegetables and the like. In fact, hurt she felt deep in the wells of her heart was neutralized and goodness was spread.

She smiled when someone told her, "thank you, for the delicious blueberry pie you made." My mother would say, "it was made especially for you and your family." The happiness she felt in performing a good deed negated the hurt her heart was feeling. It was a nurturing process all her own. We all have our own nurturing process to help us through our earthly difficult times.

Each heart is different from a heart of another person because every heart was created by our Divine God who especially felt that every human was unique and very special. Our heart has a special pathway to God's heart, and this pathway, too, is different one from the other. If we want to, it is possible to reach out to the celestial realms in a moment. The angels will hear us and respond. God will hear and will react to our concern in a manner which will make us feel better instantaneously.

All we do and experience fills our heart completely with pure love. We will truly recognize who we truly are. We inevitably knew who we were when we waited in the heavens to come to earth. To know this is important if we want to leave our mark of goodness on humanity. Everyone has something to offer humanity or else they would still be in the heavens waiting for the right time for them to enter our earthly planet.

Our heart is nurtured as is our soul through the challenges of life as it was meant to be that way. No challenge which comes our way has any weight to frighten us but rather it will strengthen our heart and our entire physical self.

There are several parts to life and afterlife and reincarnation. The heart is the part of the physical self which attracts and gives love. It wants to do everything possible to carry forth the notion that love exists in us, in the animal kingdom, vegetation, and even the tiniest particle on this earth. The heart is constantly working as a love agent in promoting such ideas. That part of our physical self yearns for everyone to have that which will enrich their lives. It wants to teach, to acknowledge, to reciprocate, to honor all there is in life in the most loving of ways.

Our heart is the closest to the celestial realms and Divine God. We may not realize it, but the great light that shines in our God is the same light that shines in our hearts. This noble light becomes brighter when we are able to bring another individual to a state of happiness, or if we do some tiny deed for humanity as a whole. Our own contentment stands in place preciously when the heart manifests such worthy experiences. It is the truth which dictates the happiness of others and is our happiness as well. This is why it's always important to remember that doing is central in bringing about a state which lives on in us.

All experiences tend to bring happiness to the heart. One may ask, even the so-called negative ones? As we have previously mentioned, experiences are just that, experiences. They are neither good nor bad, positive or negative as we have been taught to believe. Experiences of all varieties and intensities give our hearts a dedicated chance to be of service to ourselves or to others. This is what it was all meant to be. Selfishness towards others does not fit into life's equation if an individual is seeking a glowing life of enrichment.

Outstanding happenings will surround our life and those we love if this attitude is adopted on a daily basis. To make it an easier process to follow, it is well advised to identify and accept this essential aspect of spiritual living. It is a philosophy which, given thought, will find that area of one's heart which wants to respond in that manner. Your heart will enlarge not only to that of the Ages but also to that of the current now.

Your heart will have a way of vocalizing in a most loving and divine way that it is so. When you do become aware of this very special hallowed area of your heart, a profound sense of peace will overcome you. And the more you do to bring others to a state of happiness and humanity in general, the greater this area of your heart becomes. The peace will be so Divine as our Divine God's peace is. There will be no disruptions to this enchanting and glorious peace and it is possible for each person to reach that celestial state.

When there is that sacred peace in one's heart, acceptance of all matters will become very much easier. We will have a distinct grasp of what's necessary in our day-to day-activities. There will be an outline in our mind as to how to lovingly treat others on a daily basis. We will constantly ask what it is that we can do for humanity in this current now. It doesn't matter what it is, as all deeds are magnificent. What matters is that we are doing something for others.

In the past we may have considered certain situations as being problems which zapped us of energy and hope. This will no longer be the case. We will be able to handle and manage all situations with a Divine and loving message which will come from our heart. We will, in fact, begin to see all matters as being relevant but not overpowering. They will be equal and therefore will not wear us down with stress or other emotional difficulties.

Yet, within all of this, we will have the ability to offer love. Our feelings will be weighed on a scale of love and so will our interactions with others. The need for hatred, animosity, jealousy, and so forth will no longer exist, for in our Divineness we realize those attributes get us nowhere. It is only love which comes directly from the wells of our heart that matters. This is highly dependent on the plan we drew up before we came to earth as well as the approach in which our life is unfolding on a day-to-day basis.

Many of us, while still in the heavenly realms before reaching out to earth, wanted this written up in our plan and we did so. Some of us here now who didn't are finding out through the beauty of our planet and its inhabitants that love, indeed, is what we want to follow in our days on this earth. Nothing is engraved in stone, and minor adjustments are always made! Major ones are to be applauded.

Most of the Archangels have lived on earth as ordinary people so they could find out that which was lacking, why it was lacking, and what could be done about it. They worked as farmers, factory workers, librarians, teachers, mechanics, supermarket can stackers, lawyers, religious clergy, physicians and so many more occupations.

This is one reason they are so good at helping humans, because they have experienced what the humans sometimes refer to as 'their dilemma' in life.

Our beloved Archangel Raphael, for example, was on earth so many times as the healer and physician who was there and whispered in the ears of our researchers that which might help humanity in terms of procedural issues and discovery of medications.

Archangel Raphael will come to earth to be by the side of a sick person when asked to do so. He will be there when surgery is necessary and through difficult times of chemotherapy. Some of us may not know it but Archangel Raphael enlists for us all there is so that we would become healthy and offer our society that which it needs most, love! There is no request any of the Angels or Archangels will ever refuse an individual if and when they are asked. It enhances their own growth process as it does ours. Love works in the same manner for them as it does for us. There is a definite intertwining between the celestial and world realms. Our Divine God, who is a loving Divine God, works in the same manner with the celestial realms as he does with the earth and its people. There is no favoritism or unfair social class system. There is but love on all fronts!

Some of us may think we will never reach the state of complete love. This is a falsehood based on misrepresentation we have been given by some persons we come into contact with. They, at times, shame us into feeling inferior, yet we are all of the same Divine God. They want us to believe that only a few make up the rules of the game and everyone else follows. This is the farthest from the truth because when utilizing love as the ultimate there are no stern rules. Love calls only for further love. That's why it is so important to understand the concept that our Divine God wanted us to. God and his Divine workers in the striking celestial kingdom exchange situations only with love.

Divine Love will not ever stop meshing in our hearts.

— 6 —

ONE WITH GOD AND
ALL OF HUMANKIND

In the Oneness Pentecostal doctrine, there are some strong beliefs that 1. God exists and is perfect. 2. The Holy Bible as we know it was inspired by God. 3. Scripture interprets Scripture, and this in turn leads to the assertions by the Oneness Pentecostalism theology that: the Bible is the final authority; it necessitates doctrine and theology to take the entire Bible into consideration, using Scripture to translate additional Scriptures; anyone who contradicts this edict is in error.

Oneness Doctrine churches believe God is One and that God is an invisible Spirit which may only be seen in the burning bush which God creates and manifests. Jesus is the one and only begotten son of God. Oneness in this doctrine rejects the notion that any individual can become like God, either by their deeds or kindness. They further articulate that Jesus did not obtain the God eminence but rather that Jesus was manifested by God. This doctrine further believes that oneness means that God is One and not made of physical components.

In Christian thought, God is seen as a simple being and is not made up of thing upon other thing. Because he is thought of as being a simple entity, God is goodness. In Christianity, divine simplicity doesn't rule out the attributes of God as being distinguishable. One can therefore easily say God is both just and loving. Thomas Aquinas, who wrote, "Summa Theologiae implies that God appears only to the finite mind. God is present in his entirety wherever he is present, if in fact he is present anywhere. God is simple as disparate to being an entity of form and matter, body and soul and so forth. Divine simplicity allows for an abstract distinction involving the person of God, the attribute of goodness. Divine simplicity may also be synonymous with Divine Oneness in this thought."

In the philosophy of Jewish thought, Divine simplicity is addressed by the attributes of God. This was especially true with Jewish philosophers within the Muslim influence such a Sadia Gaon and Yebuda Halevi. Others identify God as creating heaven and earth (Genesis 1:1). In this thinking, God is disconnected from our Earth and thereby free of any chattels.

Divine Unity helps to understand the idea of Divine simplicity. Bahya ibn Paquda (Duties of the Heart 1:8) remarks that God's oneness is "true oneness." This idea was developed by him to indicate that an entity such as God is free of properties and thereby not describable. Thus, God is oftentimes referred to as a celestial entity of oneness. It may be entertained that this oneness is unique, like no other in creation.

Another approach concedes that Oneness is All and All can be One.

They further believe that One is a state of becoming, or that All that we are and One are the same. Eventually, given time, it is proposed that everything becomes One.

There are expressions in all religions which are similar. A few examples are given below from the so called Golden Principle. This in a very real sense represents Oneness.

Hurt not others with that which pains yourself. Buddhism, Udanavarga 5.8

Treat others as thou wouldst be treated yourself. Sikhism, Guru Angad, Macauliffe, vol2, p.29

Do unto others as you would have them do unto you, for this is the law of the prophets. Christianity, Matthew 7:12, Luke 6:31

This is the sum of all true righteousness – Treat others as thou wouldst thyself be treated. Do nothing to thy neighbor, which hereafter thou wouldst not have thy neighbor do to thee. Hinduism, Mahabharata, Ganguli, Book 13 CXIII

Another clear example of Oneness would be in the following scriptures having to do with Love Thy Neighbor:

Thou shalt love they neighbor as thyself. Judism, Leviticus 19:18

Full of love for all things in the world, practicing virtue in order to benefit others, this man alone is happy. Buddhism, Dhammapada

A new commandment I give to you. That you love one another; even as I have loved you. By this all men will know that you are my disciples, if you have love for one another. Christianity, John 13:34-35.

No one is a believer until he loves for his neighbor, and for his brother, what he loves for himself. Islam, Hadith

A third example of oneness has to do with the World Being Our Family:

Have we not all one father? hath not one God created us? Why do we deal treacherously every man against his brother? Judaism, Malachi 2:10

God hath made of one blood all nations of men. Christianity, Acts 17:26

All creatures are the family of God; and he is the most beloved of God who does most good to His family. Islam, Hadith

All are the sons and daughters of God, good people all, Brothers and Sisters, since created by One Father. No rooted difference is there between them. Hinduism, Bhavishya Purana, LLL, IV, Ch.23.

Edgar Cayce believed in one God and all of humanity as being children of that one God. Because there is only one God, who is the force behind all that exists, it follows that the Universe is created by that only one force. All things have a relationship to each other. Every individual has a definite connection to another human being, to all that exists, and to God. This great force works to bring spirituality to our world as sought by our loving Creator. With regard to spirituality, Oneness means God has no limitations as far as expressing through one religion alone. Our Divine God manifests in peoples' lives because of their faith, not because of any specific religion. Cayce believed God worked and does still work through every soul on this heavenly earth.

There are a myriad of moments in our earthly experiences that present us with a choice of path to follow in order to enhance our characteristic spiritual development.

Many options present themselves with any given

circumstance. It is up to us to choose that which helps us to magnify the All, for that is important both for the physical self and soul.

Everyone has had occasions where they later wondered why a certain feat was not taken over another to benefit the All. When asked, guidance is ours at any given time from the higher realms. It is an organized guidance which, if followed, will allow us to help the All for the benefit of all humanity. We are all participants in this glorious and sacred and loving endeavor if we so desire.

All, in spiritual and loving terms, means every human being on our earthly planet irregardless of race, religion, or beliefs is equal and loving. There is a supreme goal for each of us to follow. It is safe to assume most humans put this in their plan while still in the heavens planning to come to earth. It is an important aspect of all our lives and to be considered a great achievement even to try adding love to All.

All by itself is superfluous! It is meaningless! When we are part of the All as such, our lives are not dedicated. We are wandering through life like wild animals, not knowing what is best for our families, friends, and ourselves. It is a path with no growth. Foolish are those who claim All is the most important, for it only represents many. It also represents separation of sorts.

It is very possible to choose a spiritual path for oneself which will take the All one comes into contact with and change it to One. This is a unique loving experience such that when it occurs we will acquire the true beauty of subsistence, Love will flow easily and rapidly from your brothers and sisters on this earthly planet. It is every individual's aspiration, hope, loving desire to truly allow the All to exist and flourish as One. It is a process used by many, even though they may not be aware of it. It is something we want to embrace as our soul, yes, our soul, tells us it is a loving pathway to choose.

The soul plays a very strong and important role in our accessing the All and bringing it to One. For in the heart there speaks a voice directly from the soul which is moderate but stable for this change.

The soul, the physical self and the heart, play a large role in our own advancement to embodying All into One. This, of course, is intermingled with love. In the heart of each individual rests the power and enrichment and love which allows the All to become One. The soul through the heart sends beautiful messages that our physical self understands and wants to act upon. Further, it is believed this is where the enrichment of life which brings an individual to the ultimate, that which is Joy, is located.

Whether we know it or not, each one of us wants to follow a divine spiritual path. So many of us, at this particular time in history, want to work spiritually for humanity which has the end result of making our own lives better. It is without any question that our Divine God is ready and willing to walk the path with us, to show us the way to truly find ourselves in dedication to humanity.

Let's begin with Ascended Master Hilarion's story. The first incarnation that seems to be recorded was when Hilarion was incarnated as the Apostle Paul of Tarsus in the New Testament. He was an educated intellectual man, whose name was Saul before he became a Christian. He was taught Jewish law by Gamaliel, considered one of the great scholars of the time. At first he persecuted Christians, but then he converted to Christianity after having a vision. Subsequently he became one of the greatest apostles. His great apostolic mission was to deliver sermons throughout the Middle East and Asia. When he was in Arabia, he received direct teachings from Jesus in the Holy Land. He wrote many of the books in the New Testament. Through his preaching, he had a tremendous following. His life and ministry are of great importance to the early development of Christianity.

He did not, however, ascend at the end of his apostolic life. The reason was that he had persecuted Christians and watched the stoning of Saint Stephen, the first known Christian sufferer.

Paul's soul was reincarnated as Saint Hilarion who died around 371 Common Era (C.E.). Hilarion continued the apostolic mission he had started as Paul and this balanced the karma for his having persecuted Christians. The time he spent in the desert in Egypt was productive, as he healed thousands. The masses followed him everywhere and at the end of this life, Hilarion made his ascension. Hilarion's story may be considered a great one on all fronts, particularly in bringing the All to One.

Mother Teresa was born in Skopje, Macedonia. By the age of twelve she had God's calling to do missionary work by healing and loving. When eighteen, she left home and joined the order of the Sisters of Loreto. This was an Irish order that conducted work in India. It was in India that she took her vows as a nun and was assigned to teach but when she saw the poverty and suffering in the streets of Calcutta, something stirred deeply within her heart.

She received permission to leave the convent and work with the poor.

There was no money, of course, but she opened an open-air school for the poor children.

Volunteers helped and money donations happened. Mother Teresa started her own order of nuns called,

"The Missionaries of Charity," who would help with this gigantic task of working and helping the poor. It's worthy to note that by 1965, this order became an international religious family. Mother Teresa's missionary work spread all over the world, helping those with various afflictions such as Aids and alcoholism, and disasters, such as floods, earthquakes and famine.

Perhaps Mother Teresa is a great and loving example of bringing the All to One. She worked tirelessly on behalf of those ill and less fortunate and she too had a beautiful following which enabled All into Oneness. It is written that even in those moments where she herself was ill, Mother Teresa never gave up. Her love flowing directly from the deepness of her heart, guided by the soul, aided the thousands upon thousands less fortunate. And those persons, too, her followers, went out there in the world and in the midst of their work with others, witnessed the All become One.

Pope John Paul II was born Karol Jozef Wojtyla in Wadowice, Poland, the youngest of three children. His mother, Emilia Kaczorowska died in 1929 when he was only nine. His brother, a doctor, died when he was twelve. His father supported him so that he could study. After high school, he enrolled in Jagiellonian University in Krakow. He wanted to become an actor and did some acting and wrote plays.

When the Germans occupied Poland it s believed the then Karol Wojtyla was knocked over by a German truck. He was surprised not to be treated badly by the German officers who sent him to a hospital where he recovered from head and shoulder injuries.

It was then he decided on the priesthood.

The Germans left Poland on January 17, 1945. That

month Wojtyla helped a fourteen-year-old Jewish refugee named Edith Zierer, who collapsed from hunger while trying to reach her parents. He fed her and assisted her to the railway station. She had not heard from him again until the day he was elected Pope. Wojtyla returned to the seminary and was ordained a priest on November 1, 1946. By the time he became a priest, he lost everyone in his family, which included a sister, brother, mother and father.

In 1958 at age 38, he became the youngest bishop in Poland. In 1963 Bishop Wojtyla became Archbishop of Krakow. And, in June of 1967 he was promoted to the Sacred College of Cardinals.

Pope John Paul II had a charisma about him which immediately brought All to Oneness. Although all of us don't have the charisma of John Paul II, but we do have a charisma which is unique to us, as that's the way our Divine God wanted it. Pope John Paul II most likely had a desire to see the entire world become lovingly One. His mission took him to the far corners of the earth. He was emulated not for his charisma but rather for his message of love. It was such a strong message from the deepest wells of his heart that it reached a live audience as well as a TV audience. Young and old equally responded to this man. The transformation from the All to One was remarkable wherever he went.

And by the way, the above examples clearly show us how these magnificent beings utilized love and loving ways for the All to become One.

It is believed that in the ensuing years we will come upon a time when among other things that matter, there will be a greater release of All to One. Our Divine God, the supreme One, very much wants to join with every individual on this earthly planet in holy Oneness because God created all of us to be equal. The celestial realms will also play a major role in this magnetic transformation. Many more angels and archangels will come to earth and dwell amongst us living holy and loving lives as humans.

It is worth mentioning that even these sacred persons had setbacks of one kind or another, but that didn't bother them. They overcame the setbacks in loving style. As they, we all may have setbacks or disappointments that weigh us down with heaviness. Yet, these are mostly temporary; and with a definite concrete strategy, these disappointments will disappear and we will be back on track once again. The soul always comes to the rescue of the physical self through the heart area.

If we have such deliberate delays, disappointments, or hurts that tells we are not working toward Oneness, it need not be taken with deep wounds. The love in us that we want to extend to humanity will come forth either with the help of the soul, or through an Angel or our Divine God. The goal is magnanimous for us, filled only with love. We must allow love to take over and do its job.

Since we are unique in ourselves, created inimitably by the Divine God each to have all our own characteristics, emotions, cells, DNA and soul, it is imperative to say that each individual may find his or her own way of bringing the All to One. Someone may do this through their work as a teacher, minister, writer, factory worker, florist, lawyer, contractor or whatever that person is. Whatever that person is, is deeply embedded in a way by our Divine God. Bringing about Oneness is what was meant to be in this world of ours so that everyone equally may enjoy an enriched life and at the same time contribute to all of humanity.

If efforts are made by all individuals to bring the All to One, what a magnificent world it would be. For each and everyone of us has something to offer the All in bringing it to One. The groups of All would slowly become One until finally everything turned to One. It is possible for this to happen for this is what our Divine God wants for us, as do all those great beings in the celestial realms. Then, at last, once and for all, a total and complete Oneness with our Divine God would happen. What magnificence! What love!

— 7 —

THE JOY DIVINE LOVE BRINGS

You, each and every one of you, are love. This is what our beloved Archangel Raphael tells us over and over again. Our Divine God and the Angels want you to know that the tranquil love of the ages is all about you, with you, and for you. It is those in the celestial realms who wish it to be so, and they will do all possible to make this happen. Coming soon is a new era. In this magnificent era called Age of the Loving Astral by Archangel Raphael, there will be a beginning of experiences which will be loving, leading to a time during which love will dominate for the ultimate good of every human and all humankind.

There will be no hasty moments of anguish, but if such moments do appear they will be completely annulled by love. Each day will bring new loving challenges but these are the type you will have deep affection for. They will touch your very heart and make a lasting imprint on your soul, too. Serenity will show its happy face in the endeavors at hand. Humans will find a majestic deepness in their own serenity. In moments of anguish, if there are any, they will be sustained with serenity. Empty endeavors will be entirely filled with serenity.

Serenity will bring you closer to other human beings. It will also guide you through the challenges of love and will never be referred to as ugly challenges, or impossible challenges, or challenges you don't want in your life. Serenity will offer many possibilities for faithful actions to benefit humanity. Truthful actions will fill a human with even more love than imagined.

Serenity that is you is tenderly answerable for nourishing the soul to an outstanding importance that in so doing will lay a faithful underpinning for the many loving turning points that will present themselves in the current now and all future nows for all individuals. To understand serenity as it applies specifically to you is very important for in its truest sense it revolves around an individual's daily experiences. These experiences may be filled with love, emanating nourishment for the soul and physical self.

The serenity of our heart region is perhaps the most treasured aspect of love to an individual. It is so because the heart to most of us designates something very special in our lives here on earth. It is this attribute which will provide us with loving knowledge, wisdom, and greatness in creating the kind of world which will enrich our lives and those of all individuals. Serenity can reach a level which you will see through your third eye chakra. It will extend to the ends of the earth covering all significant points.

Serenity of purpose is glorious. It reflects you, which wants to give and give to each and every individual something which will make them happy, and it begs to offer humanity something special too. The positive and loving thing about serenity of purpose is that it works in all situations, all things, all matters, no matter what! Truthful, loving words carry with them the power of energies that emerge from the celestial realms. They offer the very best to all individuals, creatures, and vegetation of this our world. To speak such words to a brother or a sister is loving and will nourish the soul and replenish the body on a daily basis.

Serenity in a very real sense is a celebration of all individuals, creatures and vegetation. Archangel Raphael stands firmly on a mountain and states to all, "You Are Love." He further says, "Hear me, dearest friends, and believe it! For if you do, you will have awakened to love! And, if you are awakened to love, all that you desire for yourself, your loved ones, those you know, those you don't know, and all of humanity, will be possible."

The Age of Innocence was a time thousands of years ago. It was so called by Archangel Raphael. In many channelings with our beloved Archangel, it is strongly believed that he was on earth during the Age of Innocence. He speaks about it all the time! He clearly describes the Age of Innocence as a time like no other, and it is predicted we will have some semblance of it, come The Age of the Loving Astral and beyond. Archangel Raphael explains innocence as used in The Age of Innocence is related to the body, soul and heart. A Being enters our earthly planet with an innocence of all three. That innocence doesn't necessarily leave a person when that individual reaches a certain age. It may remain with a person until the moment of transition and even beyond. Innocence exemplifies a very strong love. The key to Joy is for love to remain in a human's physical self, soul, and heart.

If we are able to nourish this love, all experiences will become riches for they will be very fulfilling. If there is not this love, then anxiety, fear, loneliness, hatred, jealousy to mention a few characteristics, will take over and put us in a box. If for one reason or the other an individual loses innocence, can it be regained? The answer is unequivocally yes! It is not difficult! Sincerity, pure intent, and a fervent desire for love to return will allow it to happen. A human needs to be open to love in the current now and all future nows.

The Age of Innocence was a magnificent age during which time all brothers and sisters, everyone, had a commonality of purpose. It was helping one another that was important. All peoples were concerned for the happiness of others. Individuals supported and assisted other individuals. Families assisted and supported other families, all in the name of love and loving ways. As a result, words like prosperity or abundance had no need to ever be mentioned. They were always there!

Loving support came in many different ways: through kind words, loving deeds and actions, special or unique assistance, whatever it was a particular situation warranted. The Age of Innocence provided leadership and help on all levels of human daily experience. There was a nearness of All which formed the bond of One.

The Age of Innocence may be described as love, total love, and it could be called The Age of Love. Our planet has been altering through many magnificent alignments which will eventually benefit the experiences of all life. It is such a loving period to be here on earth as we are coming into the Age of the Loving Astral as Raphael refers to it. Some refer to it as the Golden Age of Innocence. Still others simply refer to it as the Golden Age. From all loving celestial testimonials, including that of our Divine

God, it is the time for the return to the ways of the Age of Innocence. Most humans are ready!

During the Age of Innocence as Archangel Raphael refers to it, there were many men and women called Nyorai. They were busy and worked in what was then called the Service of Love. That was their primary task in addition to other duties. The Service of Love encompassed most areas of life. Nyorai lovingly supported those who needed it most. There were many during that time who were frightened. There were some who found difficulty in living a life of love which abounded in Joy. It might have had something to do with a past life. These individuals may have experienced chaos, hurt, and discomfort before.

The Nyorai worked with these individuals. Tensions were lessened to open the heart and allow love to flow and fill the person. This was referred to as removal of blocks. After this process was over, and sometimes it took a long time, they integrated into the Age of Innocence quite nicely. Love spread from them into the ones they most loved, their spouses, then their children, and lastly into all of humanity for a better world.

Some of the Nyorai worked with Venusians who migrated to Planet Earth at that time. Venusians were admired as they were stunningly beautiful in the physical sense. Not only did they have beauty, but they had an enormous intellect.

They knew about farming, building, medicine, education and all areas of living.

Ideas were exchanged, and in so doing, both sides learned a lot. Venusians shared the concept of love as the dominant requirement for an enriched life. They were welcomed on earth and integrated into the culture of the times easily.

Our beloved Archangel Raphael revealed in some channeled material that he was a Nyorai. As such, he worked with other Nyorai to help the frightened. His work with the Venusions helped him in his own efforts of exploring and creating new ways of farming and building.

The Age of Innocence as it is told by our beloved Archangel Raphael was a time during which very many celestial beings: Angels, Archangels, spirit guides came to earth and took on human life. It was claimed to be a sacred learning experience for them. Archangel Raphael describes working at many different jobs. As a human he loved to work with his hands, and this included farming and experimenting with seeds, the growth process of vegetables, and fruit trees. Raphael wanted abundance in these areas and worked tirelessly to embark on new missions of growing vegetables to bring gigantic harvests, never losing site of the loving side of growing vegetables. He truly felt that a combination of love and intelligence would promote all around bountiful harvests and thus a healthier and more loving population.

In one of his messages, Archangel Raphael tells about the time he was on earth during the Age of Innocence and the farmers of the time worked day in and day out from early dawn until sunset to grow crops that would bring about an abundance of food for themselves and their families. Also, they wanted to help other townspeople who worked on other phases of the village and had little time for growing vegetables and working with farm animals. Raphael noticed the farmers used a method, though loving, that was taking them longer to achieve their goals. He taught them how to first grow seedlings, and when the seedlings were a certain size, they were then put in the ground and lovingly cared for to bring about huge harvests. They followed the ways of Raphael and were very pleased when at the end of the season there were still vegetables left.

Archangel Raphael introduced them to a method of saving the vegetables, similar to what is known today, as a canning process. The vegetables were preserved in huge containers with special herbs and water to keep them just as fresh as they were before the canning process. These barrels of vegetables were stored and freely given to anyone who wished them.

Our beloved Raphael also taught them about thinning fruit trees for a greater yield of fruits. He had meetings with all those interested, and they discussed certain ways to use herbs which grew freely in the woods so that insects would not destroy fruit trees or their crops. The townspeople never suspected Raphael was truly Archangel Raphael. They only believed he was a knowledgeable man who was one of the great Nyorai, ready and willing to help everyone.

Archangel Raphael also liked to build things using his hands. He would work energetically to cut trees down. It was important to have the trees cut into various sizes of boards so that small living compartments would be built. Raphael was very innovative in creating new equipment to make this process easier and more loving. He told the story of a Venusian couple who very much wanted to have their own tiny home. In those days they were referred to as compartments, rather than homes. The woman, very beautiful, known as Kimmel, was with child and told not to work until after their child was born. This was to be their first child. Her husband whose name was Magush, was a young townsperson.

They met when the Venusians landed their space apparatus. Magush told her the very moment he laid his eyes on her that he fell in love with her. Kimmel took her time. After all, this was a new land she came to. She wanted to take things slow, to integrate, and be of help where she could. Nonetheless, it happened that she could no longer hold her feelings for Magush back. She told him that he was the man for her, and she wanted a binding ceremony. A binding ceremony was similar to our marriage ceremony of the current now. They asked Archangel Raphael to officiate at this holy ceremony to join two people who loved beyond the extremes of love. They could not wait any longer to be joined together forever. As Archangel Raphael tells the story, he invited many Angels and Archangels from the celestial realms to attend. It was grand! The binding ceremony reached their very souls! They knew at the time life would be Joy! They had reached the time of Joy!

Archangel Raphael and many of the townspeople helped Magush build their tiny compartment. It was lovely in their eyes though in reality it had lacked many items such as furniture and bedding to mention but a few. It is believed that there was a day, a most beautiful sunny day, when Magush was at his regular job and away from his tiny compartment. Kimmel had been away, too, visiting with her family. When they both returned to their little compartment, it was completely furnished in the tradition of those glorious days of the Age of Innocence. Who brought all of these love items to us? They laughed as they tried to figure it out. Archangel Raphael knew all along it was the Angels who came to earth to enrich the lives of this young couple.

Magush and Kimmel were expecting their first child shortly after their binding ceremony. They had rejoiced beyond reason, as Raphael put it. A baby son was born to them. Even though Kimmel had a long labor process, she applied love to every pain she felt until a beautiful child, with its own definite plan, came into the world and was going to live during the Age of Innocence.

Raphael, known as the Angelic Healer, took a great part in the medicine of that Age which consisted of many delicate herbs and certain mushrooms. Raphael experimented with other vegetation and had spectacular results in healing of illnesses. It is believed that what Raphael began way back then is a beautiful loving backdrop to modern medicine. Archangel Raphael never wanted anyone to be ill. If a case of illness was reported, he would oftentimes remain with the person until the illness dissipated and the individual regained all the love once again. Archangel Raphael used his hands for healing as well. He would lovingly lay his hands on a person's hurtful area, and lovingly ask the person to be totally and completely healed. Marvelous healing occurred and that is why he is so sought after today for his healing abilities.

Mother Mary, Archangel Raphael's beloved partner, came to earth during that period of time as well. Mother Mary's background in healing was vast. She served as a priestess in the Temple of Truth. Her job was to take care of the fires of the Emerald Fifth Ray. This ray like the others are known to be energy from our Divine God. They radiate their magnificence to earth, touching the hearts of each individual and humanity as a whole. Mother Mary studied healing during her stay at the Temple of Truth. It was her observation that disease and cessation of life were caused by stoppages of Light into the four lesser bodies of an individual. She deducted this was due to the misuse of the Sacred Fire.

Mother Mary's days in the Temple were extraordinarily

busy. She put her total being into discovering that treatment for disease came from harmony of the flow of Light which activated the lower four bodies. She also experimented with the laws of flow that govern precipitation. Mother Mary used herself in some of these experiments, especially when it came to our Divine God's Light that healing was focused on. Although Archangel Raphael's methods and those of Mother Mary differed in some aspects, they both worked vigorously, and still do, to eradicate disease from our earth.

In today's modern era of medical advances, let it be known that Archangel Raphael is very involved in the research today whether it is in new medical machinery for testing of the human body, research for new medications, or activities in the areas of rehabilitation. He comes to earth very often and assists researchers to this end in a way that is loving, yet not known to the research doctors that it is he, Archangel Raphael, who is helping. If asked by a person who requires surgery, Raphael will be there during a major surgery to be sure the surgeon uses the correct procedure. It is important that the proper medication be used in the most difficult of cases, and Archangel Raphael is right there guiding the physicians to that end. There are those times, too, when Archangel Raphael will actually assume the role of physician or researcher should a case merit his care. He will come to earth, assume the role of a physician and operate on the individual, and while he is on earth, he may operate on hundreds of individuals using his special skills and knowledge of medicine. Archangel Raphael loves all of humanity, and there isn't anything he wouldn't do to make the world a better place.

To live an enriched life several things are important to note. It is imperative to be awakened to the fact that an enriched life is one filled with total and complete love. Life situations will always be explored and answers will come to us if we are truthful to ourselves and all of humanity in using love and loving ways to solve issues. Situations that arise may be resolved in this manner without undue conflict, anger, jealousy, or hatred.

Our state of mind will be largely uplifted for our own loving life. Humans are very strong! We may be like the great Nyorai of times gone by and that strength will also sustain us and add more love to our physical self, soul, heart, and overflow into the world. The experiences that we have in this current now may be used as practice for the new Age of Loving Astral which will soon arrive.

When we are awakened to love, our personal situations, relationships, day-to-day issues will be resolved calmly and peacefully. Our soul will be nourished! We will experience serenity! Awakening is the first step in the realization that pure love in all situations is a marvelous opportunity. Those on the spiritual path who wish to embark with love and loving ways may take time in meditation, yoga, and methods of quiet to ponder this avenue.

There is no doubt an individual may ask, "How will I grow spiritually?" You Are Love so there is no need for anyone to reiterate an answer for you. It will come to you immediately! The question may not even arise for you.

It is quite relevant to think of all the important things life: spouse or partner, children, parents, siblings, friends, a good job, some achievement you are proud of. This will not take you long. Take the thought and move it to your heart area and notice the warmth and love in your heart. It will then spread to your entire body What a pure love you are encompassed in.

A situation will no doubt come to you in thought form

where it would be appropriate to utilize love and loving ways to resolve it. Think about it! How can this situation be resolute with love? It is possible. After a fashion, a few options come to you. Decide on one that is most comfortable. Whichever one you decide on will be the right one for you. A feeling of pure love overwhelms your very being. Love and loving ways may always be used as guidance and part of a solution.

It is vital to see things as they really are and to put a little love into each situation that occurs. This holds true in all matters. It is well to remember that in addition to love, each circumstance of life has beauty.

Beauty generally creates more love. As this new energy of beauty and love combined is utilized, a new world is being created. We all have our special likes, and these might be the ones we attach to situations which need attention. In our hearts we carry the beauty of the ages. During the Age of Innocence, the great Nyorai found that beauty within their hearts which made their lives and all of those persons living then heavenly.

There is a gentle loving nobility in beauty. All humans have characteristics of uniqueness, beauty and love. If you take a walk in a commons or other so designated area, you will no doubt notice flowers, trees, bushes, birds, and all of nature's vegetation. Beauty may mean different things to different people, yet the basic concept of beauty is all around us.

In one afternoon we can experience so much to include a sunny day or a rainy day, or a snowy day. They all have beauty. As you walk and enjoy all segments of nature that our Divine God has created you will realize it is such a great privilege to be on this earth and to be able to enjoy the lavish beauty of it. It is even more spectacular to be able to contribute to beauty. Each may do this in their own special way after time is taken to find those challenges which are most dear to our hearts and the hearts of the many.

Some may play the flute to entertain masses that fill a stadium. Others like to tinker and repair machinery which is a helpful feat for another individual. Still someone else may like to sing or act and entertain the multitudes. Teachers, doctors, lawyers, tool shop workers, factory workers, car mechanics, janitors all have something noble to offer all of humanity. Everyone is talented! Our Divine loving God created every one of us with some special talent, which if utilized to the fullest, would most definitely enrich the lives of others.

If we want to explore areas which we feel are not known to us, this is possible as well. The love that is deep within us, the one that runs to the depths of our hearts and souls, and finds itself reaching out towards the ends of the earth from all sides, is equipped to perform such astounding duties if we ourselves wish it to be.

Some individuals feel they are not good at anything to put it bluntly. This, of course, is the furthest from the truth. Our Divine God has endowed each individual with everything which serves themselves, their loved ones, family, friends, co-workers and humanity in general. It's a matter of accepting and awakening to this very loving truthful fact.

It is so important to rid ourselves of any and all negatives we are trapped in. Given below are true stories (names changed) which reflect different kinds of negativity. As you read these short stories you will recognize the categories of negativity they belong to. Some have more than one form of negativity.

Negativity may stay with us from the time we were

children. Another child may say something unkind to us and we are hurt by this and right away think of it as a negative action. I remember one girl called Tess. She was a pretty girl; with dark hair, and a very becoming smile. She was created by our Divine God and was just as good as anyone else. Yet, a few young boys would always laugh, referring to her height as that of a giraffe's. This hurt her so much; it had a terrible negative effect.

We told Tess to forget what the boys said. What really mattered was what was in her heart, but Tess wasn't able to get past this for the longest time. She cried when called a giraffe. She tried to look shorter by walking bent over. The negative feelings would come out by her saying, "Why do I have to be so tall anyhow?" Or, "I know I look horrible." Tess once told me she never looked at herself in the mirror. She was ashamed of her tallness. I told her not to allow anyone to control her in that way. I kept telling her this. Eventually, the message sunk in. One day as we were walking home from high school, Tess said to me, "You know, it's not so bad being tall." I added, "It has its advantages."

"Yes, I don't need footstools to reach those high places like my mom." We laughed. It took a long time, but the negativity she allowed someone to inflict on her was gone. We remained friends for many years. After we graduated from high school, she confided, "Bob and I fell in love in our junior year in high school. I do love him so much.

He's just a bit shorter than I am, but neither of us minds. We're going to get married after college and have a bunch of kids."

I thought about Tess and her ordeal with negativity, when I began writing this book. Although I don't see her anymore, for her plan on this our earthly planet has been completed, she did marry and have four children.

One negativity, even a small one, can lead to other negativity, for there is the cumulative effect.

Another one of my friends, Celeste, hated her job. She wanted to be an artist but as we know there is little realism in believing one can make a living being an artist. Certain specialized field of art can in fact offer a better than good living. In Celeste's case, she wanted only to do landscapes. There was no flexibility for the reality of now.

Celeste settled for a job as cashier in a grocery store. She found the work to be mundane and the time dragged for her. Each day seemed like a week. If a customer wasn't happy with something, Celeste would not try to pacify the customer but rather she would encourage an urgent unhealthy discourse with the person. This led to outright fights and eventually the manager let Celeste go.

Celeste didn't want to understand why she was let go. Instead she blamed the customer for one thing or the other. She would openly call the customer unpleasantries and this stained her being with negativity. Celeste would always recount the fact that being an artist was the most important thing in the world to her.

She fought with everyone. Her landlord was an awful man when he asked her to pay her monthly rent. Her mother was far from smart because she didn't steer her in the proper direction. The schools she attended did not have the appropriate programs of study. After many relationships she termed as a waste of time, Celeste finally found a man she fell in love with. She talked about his faults, and the marriage lasted no more than a year. She desperately wanted a child, but it didn't seem likely with this man since they had broken up. Celeste referred to him as a loser because there were no children. There was such a buildup of negativity in this woman it would take years of therapy to go through all of the things that entered her world and made her feel everyone was 'no good' or was simply 'not with her' on anything.

Celeste's story is one of negativity that was placed onto others. With that frame of mind, it would be impossible to reach any level of enrichment.

There are times when we listen to others stories of negativity, and that negative energy will reach us in a way we had never expected. So, we need to be careful in being the good listener. It is our responsibility to help others, but we must always remember to send them a loving energy and wash ourselves with love.

We all know someone who complains all the time. Nothing seems to go right for them. This is clearly a woman named Alicia. Her husband is having an affair. She apparently knows the woman as she babbles on and on about her, calls her a cow and other distasteful names. What will she do? Leave this guy? Oh, maybe she'll just put up with it; most men have affairs. Then, in the next few sentences Alicia is going to go see a lawyer and give him an earful.

Alicia talks about her oldest boy, eighteen, who won't budge to get a job nor will he go to college even though they can afford to send him. She goes into the whole thing that it's not his fault; it must be the company he keeps. They are a bad influence on him. They tell him not go to college or get a job. Because the oldest boy is going through his own thing, she believes the youngest one is lazy for that reason. She'll explain it by saying, "Sonny sees Billy laying around the house, and of course he wants to do the same thing." Then, she talks about how the two of the boys argue when they are in direct sight of each other. After she's done with her family, Alicia talks about the neighbors and what bad characters they are. It is all negative stuff! All of it!

If you know someone like this you must ask Archangel Raphael to reverse this trend to become positive with love and return it to her, in this case, Alicia, immediately. You must also ask that if any of that energy touched your person in any way, it must be immediately reversed to positivity and love.

We must be careful in this wonderful world of ours because there are people who because of their own issues want to throw, yes, throw, negativity at us. This is a very cruel type of negativity but one may shake it off and move forward to a positive and loving existence. Donna was jealous of a project that Sam was working on. Sam was very excited about the project and wanted to share it with her. But, every time Sam started to speak of it, Donna would cut him off and make small talk or do something which had no relevance whatsoever to the project.

Sam did manage to get enough information to her so that she discussed it with one of her friends without asking Sam if it were okay to do so. Apparently, Donna and her friend criticized Sam's project even though it was merely in the inception stage. Added to that, Donna told Sam she agreed with her friend's comments about the project. Her friend thought it was basically a mediocre project with no merit whatsoever. Donna had no problem telling Sam that she discussed his project with her friend and she agreed with her friend.

Sam was a gentleman so he didn't argue with her. He decided then and there that it might be a good idea for him not to see Donna for a while even though they considered each other friends.

That evening Donna called him and said to him,

"Now, I want you to listen to me. Don't say a word, just listen." Seemingly what had transpired was exceedingly unpleasant. Donna was totally off base in some of the horrible things she said to him. They both hung up without Sam being given a chance to ask any questions.

Sam sensed there was something wrong. He asked a woman who works with Archangel Michael to cleanse him, the room he was in when the phone call came, and even the pet cat. The woman did this and later called Sam. She told him that Archangel Michael cleansed him of a spewed sticky material that was all over him, the couch, and the cat.

This is a very malicious form of negativity. Fortunately, positivity and love can win over this, and the person is able to function in a loving manner towards others.

There are many forms of negativity and it's very important to rid ourselves of all the negativities. Once we do, the love our Divine God gave us will once again fill our physical bodies, souls and hearts.

Let's not be prissy with our words here; this is very important. The crap we have accumulated from our years on this earth must be dealt with in order to begin living a loving life. We will mention a few more specific forms of negativity in true story form, and they will be recognized as such.

Some youngsters are shy when they are young. There are reasons for this such as feeling inadequate, not having as much as another youngster, not feeling pretty or good looking, loss of a loved one, and many more. The picture is clear. Barbara was such a youngster who was very shy. In her case it was a feeling her parents were not able to afford to give her the kinds of things other children had. There was poverty and no money for piano or guitar lessons, singing lessons, movies, or jujitsu lessons. Barbara felt very deprived. She was the youngest in a family of nine children.

Barbara's oldest sister, Nina, was married to a man who was ruthless, vulgar, and oversexed. Because there was a lack of money, Barbara's oldest sister offered to live in the family home to help pay expenses. This created the perfect opportunity for Wilbur, Nina's husband, to constantly put his hands on Barbara, including touching her private parts. Barbara didn't know what to do. She became filled with anger! Barbara was very shy at the age of twelve and put up with Wilbur's sexual advances. One day, it had come close for Wilbur raping her, were it not for her sister coming home early from work. Barbara just cried instead of telling her sister or anyone about what was going on. The anger within her was boiling. Her mother wouldn't believe her if the truth be known, she thought, and neither would her sister or her other siblings. So, she lived a life of wretchedness accompanied by more and more anger.

A day came when Barbara blurted out to Wilbur, "I'll kill you if you ever touch me again." He laughed and his advances became even more frequent. Wilbur forced her into her bedroom one day with the intent of having sex with her. She resisted with all her might, biting him, spitting on him and kicking him in the groin area but nothing would stop this maniac. He got her on the bed, when all of a sudden Barbara's mother came into the room and caught them.

"Mommy, mommy," Barbara cried out, "he's trying to hurt me." The words came out in stuttered fashion, but her mother knew that her youngest daughter Barbara was telling the truth. Wilbur tried to explain otherwise! It was the end of the most miserable year of her life. When her sister, Nina, found out, there was a lot of deliberation, but Nina, too, acknowledged that Barbara was telling the truth.

"Mommy," Barbara told her mom, "I never wanted him to touch me. It was so ugly. I was so angry. Mommy, I am still so angry, I could kill him." Barbara's mom understood. She took her daughter in her arms and told her she loved her very much and all would be fine. She assured her over and over again. Together, Barbara and her mother went to a therapist for the longest time, until Barbara was able to move on with her life.

The above story is one which we don't want children to go through. It tells us about abuse, anger, and hatred too.

The teenage girl, Trisha, who lived next door to Rhonda and Bill was mischievous. Her parents knew this yet allowed Trisha to do more or less what she wanted. Both parents worked so there was no supervision from the time Trisha came home from school and her parents came from work. They gave her duties like preparing some of the evening meal, and Trisha at all times complained about doing what was necessary. It was only when her allowance was in jeopardy that Trisha would adhere to the rules of the household.

Trisha had many friends who were of the same type. One day they got a hold of some bright red paint. When they saw the neighbors go off, Trisha, the instigator, told the others it would be fun to go to the neighbors' and paint some red over the brown shingles.

The house next door was a lovely home, kept up and cared for. This didn't matter to either Trisha or her friends. They found an old paintbrush in the cellar of Trisha's home, opened the red paint can so the paint would be easily within reach and headed for the neighbors' home in a very nonchalant way so no one would be suspicious.

When they got there, it was Trisha who smeared the red paint all over the brown shingles. It looked horrible, to say the least. Her two friends laughed and laughed. Finally, the job was accomplished. They went back to Trisha's house as if nothing had happened. To them, it was just a fun thing to do after studying all day in school. Trisha and her friends buried the paint can and brush so there would be no evidence.

When the neighbors came home, they were devastated. They both suspected Trisha of doing this, knowing her history, yet there was no proof. The red paint remained on the house for a day or two. The neighbors hoped Trisha would own up to it but it never happened. Finally, after much stress and tension, the red was repainted to its original color of dark brown. It was not known whether or not these people ever complained to Trisha's parents. It was believed they had. This is a story about someone imposing their negativity for their own fun.

There are many other forms of negativity. It can work both ways. The sender is full of negativity and sends it to someone. Negativity may also have many components in just one incident. A few will be mentioned here: temper, jealousy, hatred, envy, depression, resentment, anxiety, being judgmental, and unforgiving. There are many more, and they all interrelate to make it a real challenge to rid oneself of this negativity.

It is possible and it is not difficult to do. Before love the Divine God gave us fills our physical bodies, our souls and our hearts once again, we must rid ourselves of the buildup of this negativity we have accumulated through the years of living. We must return to the physical self, the soul and the heart that we were born with. That was the love our Divine God breathed into us before we appeared on this earth as the tiny child. The child wanted this love to always remain, for it was the love of the ages. It was a special love, not easy to describe, but a love which could be applied to all situations for the strongest benefits possible. Living a life on earth is not an easy endeavor, and that's why so many souls take their time returning to earth.

Our beloved Archangel Raphael, too, was born through the womb of a woman when he came to live a life during the Age of Innocence. His messages reveal this was done primarily in order that he would experience the love to see whether it coincided with the love in the celestial realms. Later, as he lived and worked in the villages which comprised the Age of Innocence, he knew it was indeed the same type of love from our Master, our Lord, our Divine God. This special love is something which no one can adequately explain, but the longer one stays on this earth from birth with this love, the higher loving mentality craves for it. This higher self is better equipped to explain this phenomenon and exactly how it feels. Without a doubt there are some individuals, depending on where they live, who are able to live this love for a good number of years on our earth before being 'boxed' into negativity of others and our earth.

Many individuals on a spiritual journey have left the large cities for small country towns with few inhabitants to see if they may preserve this natural God-given love, which is our Divine right to experience. Some people living in the cities through necessity find life may still offer the opportunity for an existence of Divine love as it was when they first departed the comfort of the womb. This Divine love is one which needs no one, yet wants everyone to join in as One and work towards the common cause of love in all matters in this our earthly planet. This Divine love is persistent, and yet it somehow gets away from us no matter how much we want to drape ourselves in it.

The reasons for this have been already mentioned in this little book and they are namely of our interactions with others who also want to learn Divine love but haven't yet come to that point in their hallowed lives. Everyone wants this, whether they will admit it or not. It can be someone who argues and has the worse temper this side of the Mississippi, yet this person is looking for this special Divine love. Or, it can be the individual who was born to riches and may even feel guilty about it while those around the person suffer! Everyone is looking for this special Divine love in their lives. That is why they came to earth! They want to help and assist those already here in finding that love which was lost shortly after birth. In some cases it may have been after a few years or even several years.

It is important to note that this reflects the notion that our Divine God is a beautiful spirit which lives within all of us. He wants nothing more than to bring the All to Oneness including the celestial realms and the earth, and even possibly other planets. When we grow in love from our Divine God, the love grows ever so much stronger until all becomes possible.

It is appropriate at this time to give two prayers which will help eliminate all negativity from your physical self, soul, and heart. To be successful, and it is more than possible, one must be humble. This is very important as all of us came into this our loving world with humility. We wanted love to last! We wanted to serve humanity on a grand spectacular scale.

Our beloved Archangel Raphael has channeled the following to be used by humans to rid themselves of negativity. He understands well, as do all in the higher realms that this is not an easy task, but it may be accomplished. If you are comfortable in doing so, the following prayers are a gift from Archangel Raphael to you.

The first covers humbleness. As already stated, this is very important in bringing back the status of positivity and ridding oneself of negativity.

It is brief but extremely powerful. Archangel Raphael asks that you say the following entreaty once a day for several days. He leaves the number of days up to you.

HUMBLENESS
Divine God, Mother Mary, and all the Angels
in the celestial realms. I am happy and grateful that love
may be totally and completely mine, if I only allow
it to flow into me. It will not only engulf the entire
body but will nourish my soul and fill my heart.
I am ready to feel the love of the ages, and the
love our Divine God created me with. I appreciate
the goodness of life and want to work to make the
world a better place for all those I know, those I
don't know, those who are here now, and those who
will come after me. Thank you Divine God,
Mother Mary and all the Angels in the celestial realms
who are supporting me.
.........Archangel Raphael

The following is a brief ceremonial prayer to rid ourselves of negativity. We know it won't happen overnight! We were filled with only love when we came to this earth, and so it took many years, in some cases, to fill our bodies, souls and hearts with negativity. It will take time to reverse the process, and our Divine God and all his helpers assure us it can be done. The loving energies were handed down by our Divine God to Archangel Raphael when we need healing in a particular situation; in this case, it will work to heal negativity. This prayer a very sacred experience and cannot be taken lightly. Our beloved Archangel Raphael healed thousands of people utilizing the healing energies given to him directly from our Divine God.

The prayer has the qualities to infuse our bodies, souls and hearts with Archangel Raphael's energies and also those of our Divine God. It is wise to have someone on their spiritual path to read this payer to you. Or, it may also be transmitted by a loving person such as a family member. The person may be sitting comfortably or lying down and be alone except for the one who will read this prayer.

We ask the person relax totally. The prayer may be said at any time during the day.

A CEREMONIAL PRAYER TO PULL OUT THE THORNS OF NEGATIVITY

(You are speaking to the person's Higher Self)

(Person's Name) This prayer is very somber and serious for it deals with ridding yourself of negativity. It unfolds on a sandy area in the desert. The sun is brightly shining. It is a great and wonderful day for praying. There are a few cactus plants here and there, and the windy atmosphere smells sweet. Your nostrils fill with the wonders of this particular smell!

Angels join us and make a loving circle around us. Archangel Raphael appears as does Mother Mary. Archangel Raphael whispers into your ear and asks you if you want to rid yourself of negativity. You reply unequivocally yes.

Next, one of Raphael's Angels hands you a golden

platter. Archangel Raphael and Mother Mary touch the golden platter, then move away. You still hold the platter.

The Thorns of Negativity will now be pulled from your body, soul, and heart. Each thorn represents negativity. Raphael and Mother Mary work to gently ease all the thorns from your body, soul and heart. It takes time, but it is being done. You don't feel any pain when this is being done, but rather you feel immense relief to rid yourself of negativity.

They keep working and putting all the thorns on the golden platter. It is filled high with negativity thorns. Finally, after a long while, they have finished.

Mother Mary so announces to you. (Person's Name) You are so very happy to hear this. You thank both Archangel Raphael and Mother Mary. Archangel Raphael asks you to look at the thorns one last time for you will never see them again. Our Divine God will redirect them into love, he tells you. (Person's Name) You look at the thorns; you are still holding the golden platter.

Divine God, Mother Mary,
Archangel Raphael, Angels from the
celestial realms, I thank you for ridding
me of negativity. I feel as though my body
is flowing in love; it is that love which
I came to earth with. It is that love which
I want to enjoy for the rest of my earthly life.
Thank you, for this gift.
Amen

Now, it is time to give up the golden platter, the negativity. You no longer want it.

You no longer need it. Your life will be filled with love.

Archangel Raphael blesses the thorns before he removes the golden platter from your hands. Mother Mary places both her hands above the thorns and prays on them. Then, one of Raphael's Angels takes the platter and places it in a box. (Person's Name) It is requested by Archangel Raphael that the box be sent to the heavens where our Divine God will greet it. It is so done.

This prayer for the removal of thorns of negativity is now coming to an end.

(Person's Name) Archangel Raphael and Mother Mary will bless you before they leave for the celestial realms. They both do this. Moments later they are gone. And, the Angels have left as well. We thank Archangel Raphael, Mother Mary, and Raphael's Angels for participating in this very essential prayer.

(Person's Name) The prayer is now completed.

It is recommended that the receiver of this prayer remain in a reclining position for several moments with the facilitator by his/her side. After a few minutes have passed, the person may get up and resume their activities.

ARCHANGELS ARE
LOVING AND SUPPORTIVE

We have discussed Archangel Raphael throughout this book thus far in nearly every chapter because I am most familiar with his fabulous work for humankind. It is important to discuss the other six Archangels who everyone may find to be very caring, as they walk their loving spiritual path leading to Joy.

Archangels have experienced it all. They are capable of healing and when asked, will not ever refuse. In addition to their healing abilities, with Archangel Raphael being the Angelic Healer, they all have other areas of expertise that one may gain benefit from.

If a person is ever in doubt, or has a question, it is well to remember that our beautiful archangels are always on call. As a matter of fact, they want to be involved in making the Earth a better place. They relish the thought of an enriched life for everyone. Each of the Archangels has a huge army of Angels who work with them to see that a specific project gets done. They also have a counterpart, known as an Archeia, thus creating the male-female equilibrium.

Considered to be the most sought after Archangels are: Michael, Jophiel, Chamuel, Gabriel, Raphael, Uriel and Zadkiel. We will give below a brief informational sketch about each of these Archangels except Raphael.

ARCHANGEL MICHAEL is perhaps the most popular of the seven. His name means, "Who is Like God." Michael utilizes a soldier-like strength to protect human beings. Michael may show us different ways of dealing with difficult problems. Michael will not allow us to become distracted while trying to accomplish a goal. Though he uses a warrior technique, Michael is really full of gentleness. Archangel Michael works with Archeia Faith. It is known that Archangel Michael and Archeia Faith will not hesitate to help us manifest our greatest and most wanted desires and dreams.

Among his attributes are Will and Power. He is associated with the Heart Chakra.

If you want your home protected, ask Michael. He and Faith will protect any individual who asks, from those who may have evil intentions. Lord Michael, as he is sometimes referred to, is the guardian Angel of Israel and the protector of the Christian Church. In the Old Testament book of Daniel, there is a note that he will emerge when the world is in gigantic danger. It is also predicted that at the end of the world, Archangel Michael will combat and destroy the antichrist. In the Dead Sea Scrolls, he is known as the "Prince of Light," who battles the Sons of Darkness. It is he, the Prince of Light, who effectively leads the celestial Angels against the legions of the fallen Angel, Belial.

In 1950 Pope Pius XII accredited Archangel Michael

as the Patron Saint of policemen everywhere. Marines also look to Michael as their protector in times of battle.

Protection is the highest priority on Archangel Michael and Archeia Faith's list. They don't want to see harm of any kind come to anyone. This would not only include property and personal damage but also abuse, put downs and the like.

ARCHANGEL JOPHIEL'S name means, "Beauty of God." Jophiel brings to us the virtue of wisdom. Humans will learn how to assess their own wisdom and beauty within, appreciating the beauty and wisdom in other human beings. Working with Jophiel is Archeia Christine. Archeia Christine acts as the temple for the attribute of wisdom. Christine's help is sought by those who need a center of attention on matters relating to wisdom. With the assistance of Christine, issues become sensible. Jophiel is associated with the Crown Chakra.

Jophiel is known as the Angel of beauty. It has been written that it was Jophiel who drove Adam and Eve from the Garden of Eden. He is known to have secured the Tree of Knowledge of Good and Evil. This tree played an important role in their eviction from Eden. It has been written that when Eve took a bite of the apple, the knowledge of both evil and good emerged. Thus, the beginning of evil worked on humankind to forget what love was.

The illuminating yellow light will guide humans on their greater spiritual path.

It will allow us to understand the light within and help us in absorbing convoluted information and diverse matters. Jophiel is also recognized an expert in fighting pollution and cleaning up our earth. He has an army of

Angels lovingly referred to as the Angels of Illumination. They assist wherever they are needed, especially if they notice there is a flicker of wisdom which would lead to greater, more beautiful, loving manifestations.

Many hairdressers ask Jophiel and Christine for help in their profession, especially those who believe natural beauty is of the essence and who want to align their skills to that end.

Archangel Jophiel and Archeia Christine will always help matters relating to wisdom, beauty, and the environment.

ARCHANGEL CHAMUEL'S name means, "He Who Sees God." There have been many different variations of his name depending on the text which is read. He is sometimes known as Carmiel, Kemuel, Camiul, and Seraphiel, to mention a few. Archeia Charity is his counterpart. Their love for one another is sometimes referred to as a love which transcends all understanding. Since we've said many times in this book that our Divine God is love, Chamuel and Charity administer divine love. They exemplify the expression, "Thou shalt love the Lord thy God with all thy heart, with all thy soul, and with all thy spirit"

Archangel Chamuel brings to the Universe the virtue of adoration through the softness of his pink light or ray, as it is known. Adoration is a reverence of God, and all of God's teachings. It is through this admiration that we are committed to the goodness of life. Adoration may be shown by the stillness in our hearts, as in meditation, and this will light up the reasons for our earthly existence. He is associated with the Throat Chakra.

Chamuel and Charity are deeply concerned with relationships. We must love ourselves, first, is what they believe. They further believe in giving unconditional love to others. The love which returns to our physical self, soul, and heart will be ten-fold.

Practically everyone on this earthly planet has at one time or another been hurt by sexual love. True love has no time attached to it; no limits. It is a love directly given to us from our Divine Creator. And, our Divine God has endowed Chamuel and Charity with the capacity to understand this kind of love and to support those who need it.

Chamuel and Charity will help us in finding new loving friends, in repairing broken relationships, and generally helping humans to lovingly interact with one another

Ask Archangel Chamuel and Archeia Charity if you are having difficulty in meditating, or loving someone in a sexual relationship, or extending a humanitarian type of love to someone who may need it.

Sometimes, Archangel Chamuel and Archeia Charity are referred to as a twin pink flame which illuminates the darkness we may feel, and manifests it into light. This makes direct reference to a relationship in trouble as it might be interpreted in just that way.

ARCHANGEL GABRIEL'S name means "the power of God" or "God is my Strength." He and Archeia Hope give the world the virtue of purity in its radiant white color. Purity represents our Divine God to its highest level. Purity also represents our Divine Mind, given to us directly from God. Gabriel and Hope are also concerned with communication, harmony with self and others, perfection and love.

Except for Michael, he is the only Archangel mentioned in the Old Testament by name. It is he, Gabriel, who announces to Mary that she is to become the mother of baby Jesus. Christian art often depicts Archangel Gabriel carrying a trumpet, and kneeling before Mary announcing the birth of Jesus.

Gabriel is associated with the Base of the Spine Chakra. Jewish legend has indicated Gabriel parted the Red Sea and allowed the escape of the Hebrew people from Pharoah's soldiers. Archangel Gabriel and Archeia Hope are known to assist men and women in the ascension process, which is reuniting the soul with our Divine God. On some levels he is known to represent creation, and Gabriel is thought of as the Archangel of childbirth. Henry Wadsworth Longfellow in his poem, "The Golden Legend," refers to Gabriel as the Archangel of the moon, whose mission is to constantly bring hope to the world. Please note that his counterpart's name is Hope.

Archangel Gabriel has been known as one who beautifully interprets visions that come to the many. He is mentioned in the Story of Daniel in the Bible. Daniel has this atrocious vision of a ram stomping to the west, the north, the east, the south, and no animal was able to overtake the ram until finally, a goat did, after a severe struggle.

In 1951 Pope Pius XII declared Gabriel to be the patron saint of all those involved in the communication field, be it acting, music, writing, journalism or anything else in that field.

If you want help in these areas mentioned above, seek it of Archangel Gabriel and Archeia Hope. The "announcer," as he is known, and his counterpart, Hope, are very willing to be supportive of any of your efforts.

ARCHANGEL URIEL'S name means "Fire of God," or "God is My Light." He and Archeia Aurora represent the virtue of ministration. They are associated with the Ruby color connected to spiritual service to humanity which unites within our heart and soul. Archangel Uriel and his counterpart, Archeia Aurora, give the earthly planet the love used in veneration to all humankind, Archangel Uriel plays a major role in uniting us with our Divine God. They are both associated with the Solar Plexus Chakra whose genuine attributes are will and determination.

Archangel Uriel always endows our beautiful planet with his never ending love, which is gently accompanied by peace and safe being for all humans. He and Aurora are enthusiastic about the prospect of supporting those wanting to join God's service by schooling them to show charitability, consideration and love to all of humankind.

Their colors form a beautiful combination of transformation and forgiveness. And, the purple aspect, derived from the joining of purple and gold, creates a want for spiritual endeavors.

Archangel Uriel is known as the "regent of the sun," "the flame of God," "the Angel of Retribution," and the Archangel of Salvation" Some say it was Uriel who gave the Kabbalah, the Hebrew mystic tradition, to the world.

In Milton's, "Paradise Lost," Archangel Uriel has a role in the fall of man. Satan seeks revenge after losing a battle and being forced from heaven. He tricks Uriel into giving him directions to Earth so that he can harm God's creations, Adam and Even. Satan dressed as a cherub, fools Uriel, and gets directions to Earth from Uriel. It isn't long after that Uriel realizes he was fooled by Satan. He asks Archangel Gabriel and other Archangels and Angels to protect the first humans. According to Milton's story, however, it is too late.

Archangel Uriel has also been known as a great interpreter. In the First and Second Books of Esras, in the

Old Testament, Uriel reveals from the Hebrew Prophet Esra's visions; that a Messiah has been sent to defeat evil on earth.

Seek the help of Archangel Uriel and Archeia Aurora when you need help on your spiritual path, or if you intend to dedicate your life to our Divine God's service by helping humankind, or have difficulty in interpretation of any documents.

ARCHANGEL ZADKIEL'S name means "Angel of Freedom." He and Archeia Amethyst bring us the violet light which designates the virtue of forgiveness. They both work tirelessly to show humans the road to forgiveness. Zadkiel and Aurora have the special talent to instill all humans with the power to liberate themselves from wounds which are self-imposed. Zadkiel and Amethyst will assist anyone who wants to implement forgiveness. They both know it is difficult at times for one human being to forgive another, yet with gentle support, it is possible to do so. This forgiveness will work a long ways in turning it into love for the benefit of the forgiver.

There are situations where forgiveness may take a long time because certain issues are involved. No matter how long it takes, Archangel Zadkiel promises to work with you until an issue is resolved. If he feels the Divine God needs to intervene, Zadkiel will not hesitate to have this happen.

Zadkiel also works to free humans from pain caused through so called "mis-qualified energy" caused by negative feelings, thoughts, words, and actions.

Along with forgiveness, Archangel Zadkiel and Archeia Amethyst work to help you rid your physical self of fear. There are many different types of fear, but the good part is all fear may be manifested into love.

In all instances where you feel forgiveness is necessary or fear runs rampant, do not hesitate to seek the counsel and support of Archangel Zadkiel and Archeia Amethyst.

Given below is a short prayer to the Archangels to help us as we travel on our path of love and loving ways to heal the situations of the current now and all future nows.

The Archangels love us, and together the love of the ages will spread from them to our bodies, souls and hearts.

Archangels: Michael, Jophiel, Chamuel,
Gabriel, Raphael, Uriel and Zadkiel,
it is with a deep and lasting love in my very
being that I may occasionally ask for your assistance
and support in certain situations. My heart
is filled with a desire to do all that is necessary
to enrich my life, the lives of those I adore,
those I don't know, and all of humanity.
Amen.

There are many other Archangels who work specifically on matters which may seem to be troubling to you. The six mentioned above, and our beloved Raphael, play a very important part in all our lives as they deal with those issues which seem to come up for us often. Archangels will not ever let an individual down. They will come to earth, assume a human form, and do that which is necessary for a human to enjoy an enriched life. One may call upon another to help. They may go directly to our Divine God and summon his help, which he lovingly offers without hesitation.

— 9 —

THE PATH TO JOY

It is at this juncture important to think about what we would like to do to enrich our lives, the lives of others – those we know and those we don't know – and all of humanity. We may want to consider the following several suggestions as a starting point in our marvelous journey on the path to Joy. Many spend a lifetime in pursuit of a life which is filled with abundance, love, and a special mission. It is attainable to every human being who desires it by utilizing love and loving ways in all aspects of life. Each one of us has our own way of reaching a time when love and loving ways will dominate our lives in all we do for ourselves, those we love, and all of humanity. There is no right or wrong way to reach this goal. There will be setbacks but the steps forward will increase as we glowingly walk our path with those others who have chosen to do the same.

The first step in acquiring and keeping a life which is enriching in every way is to want it. There can be no doubt! Some individuals may weakly say they want an enriched life but to just say it in that way brings little, if no results. There must be the strong desire that an enriched life is possible. The enthusiasm for an enriched life must fill the physical body, soul, and heart so totally and completely, so much so, that nothing else matters. There will be some bits and pieces from the past which will tend to interfere with this beautiful process, but those remnants must be ignored. They will in time go away. An individual may feel not good enough for such a remarkable existence. Those thoughts, too, must fall by the wayside, as we know all humans are worthy of the very best our world has to offer. If a path of Joy is wanted, it will come about in the most divine way.

No one wants suffering in their lives. It only leads to more suffering. It wasn't meant to be that way. We all aspire to achieve the most we can for ourselves and those we love. We must always remember to include those we don't know, for they too deserve to enjoy a life that is rich and extensive, and filled with love on all levels. It is good to begin this process by lovingly healing that which may still bother us on some level, rather than moving forward carrying unwanted and unneeded baggage from the past. The past won't matter, once an individual is on the path to handling matters lovingly.

To help with this process and to begin a journey leading to an enriched life, the following brief prayer may be said to our Beloved Raphael. Your own words to Raphael will do as well.

Archangel Raphael, I feel so
happy at this very moment. An
enriched life is something
I really desire with all my heart.

Help me in any way
you can, as I begin my journey
on this noble path of love and
loving ways.
I am ready!
Amen

After you complete the prayer, sit in a comfortable chair and think about the beautiful and loving spiritual path you are to embark upon. If you are already on a spiritual path, it will become even more loving, thus making your life fulfilling each and every day.

We talked about everyone having a plan drawn up before coming to earth. It is important to identify whether or not an individual is living the plan. There are some ways to know this, and they are easily detected. If, for example, life is moving along without difficulty, most likely a plan is being followed. If a person is happy in their circumstances, it is likely a plan is followed. If a someone is loving and doesn't allow world criteria to upset them in handling situations, then, it would seem apparent the plan the person wrote up is being lovingly followed. All positivity in one's life, no matter how difficult a situation, points that a plan is in progress.

If, on the other hand, someone displays arrogance, hatred, jealousy, anger, and so forth towards another human being, or the solving of an issue, then it is not likely a plan is being followed. If a person is constantly grumpy and seeking something they don't have or displaying wishful thinking, then a plan is not progressing. If a human being develops traits which irritate others, cause problems for others, then most likely the person's plan is not being followed. If an individual says they are not ever happy, then, of course, they have lost track of their original plan.

Some persons are able to follow their plan half way. This means they go through life neither happy nor sad, neither loving or unloving; they just seem to exist because they are here on earth. There is nothing definite or concrete they can say which is of importance for them to accomplish. Their dealings with others are not hateful but, yet, show no loving signs. They may tolerate and accept what is thrown at them.

Even sadder than the just mentioned state, are those individuals who have been in some way abused in their lives. This standing remains with them throughout their lives. They feel they are not worthy of anything good, not to mention love! They want very much to love and be loved but it escaped them. Sometimes, they just put up with all matters without even a serious loving discussion about a situation. This type of person needs lots of love from others to get back on their plan. Archangel Raphael, Mother Mary and other Angels will always help.

The bottom line is this. Some individuals are following their original plan which always includes love and loving ways in handling all life situations. Others, not through their fault, have gone completely off their plan because of the world around them. Still others follow their plan to an extent, but not fully. They feel it, but don't know why they feel the way they do. The last category are those who need all the love everyone in the world can give them. Because of circumstances that happened to them after birth, they are not on their plan, and very much would like to be.

It is safe to say all humans want to be on the plan they drew up prior to coming to this earth. They want to enrich their lives and the lives of others through love and loving ways, and their own personal missions. And, the good part is that no matter where an individual is in terms of their plan, it is possible to get back on course. Those who are on their plan and who have been on their plan since birth, are the great Nyorai of today. They are the happy warriors who can help others! And that what's it's all about.

Many spiritual healers can help you to find out whether you are on your original plan or not. You will know yourself by just reading the above material. If you feel you are not on your original plan, it is not difficult to get back on it. All you need to do is ask for it to happen, and begin living the way you originally planned to live with a focus on love and loving ways. You may ask Raphael for assistance if you like. Your own words will do as well.

Beloved Archangel Raphael, I (Your Name) request
that you search all the books of life in the
celestial realms. I want to know whether
or not I am on the plan I drew up before coming
to Earth. If I am, please tell me so! If I am not,
please tell me what is lacking. What must I do to get back
on my plan which I loved so much while creating it.
It was my original plan, and that is why I decided to
come to Earth. I will await your answer!
I thank you Archangel Raphael for helping me
with this important matter.
Amen

There is the matter of first allowing oneself to awaken to the possibility that life is grand in every sense of the word. Many of us realized this valuable fact while still in the celestial realms planning our next life on this earth. Some of us came to earth with total love and something happened to dissipate this love. With the closure of the Era we are living in now and the onset of a new era, The Age of the Loving Astral, as Raphael refers to it. It seems appropriate to visit some more attributes which will allow us to live a life where love and loving ways are utilized to make us happy for the entire time we are on this our earthly planet.

Awakening to love is perhaps the most essential tool an individual may adapt, to travel an exciting spiritual path. We discussed awakening in a previous chapter but it is so very important, mention of it here once again is very appropriate. Archangel Raphael strongly believes solving matters in a loving way teaches us to disperse conflict, hatred, anger, jealousy, abusiveness, and the like. He came to earth so very many times to prove over and over that his theory of love and loving ways can, in fact, become a definite way of life for everyone.

Archangel Raphael purposely placed himself in situations in which angry tones, for example, could be displayed. He found that through love and loving ways, there was no anger; and whatever might have been felt at the outset by others, had quickly vanished. Archangel Raphael further discovered through his missionary work on this planet earth, that humans were actually seeking something they didn't have in their lives. It was as if they were waiting for someone to tell them, "try love and loving ways. It really works!"

Archangel Raphael wasted no time in spreading this truth throughout the world. By so doing he not only touched the hearts of many humans, but he also found that they were able to incorporate it into their lives to live an enriched life for the benefit of their loved ones, themselves, and all of humanity. Raphael, in his teachings, drew large crowds of thousands. He loved to teach sitting under a large tree. It didn't matter what kind of tree it was or whether it bore fruit or not, as long as it was a large tree. The crowds gathered around the tree for as far as the eye was able to see. Sometimes, a tree that was unhealthy and was unable to bear fruit, gave a rebirth, and soon was a healthy tree bearing a plentiful amount of fruit. People marveled at the experience and rejoiced in it.

Archangel Raphael was a great teacher as he was able to invoke in each and every human Being the truth that they are love. Not only that, but they are strong and up to all challenges as well. During the Age of Innocence, he often referred to humans as great Nyorai, and riders and warriors, and noble Beings of love.

In recent data, Archangel Raphael claims we are like the great Nyorai who truly lived love. He reiterated over and over again in his messages that pure love is needed to enhance personal situations, relationships, and all day-to-day issues of significance to us. If we do this, he continues, our souls, too, will be nourished. A nourished soul is an awakened soul for all time, up to our transition, and beyond.

It is vital to enjoy the beauty surrounding one's life. Take a walk and enjoy the beauty of nature. There is nothing more relaxing than listening to the tones of the various birds that occupy our area of life. The appealing birds which our Divine God created for us to enjoy, are loving, especially when they feed their young. They are teaching us something of life which brings our hearts to hum in merriment for we are learning from those marvelous little birds. When they seem hungry, we recognize it! If we feed them, there is a certain remembrance of it in our life's history. Birds have a way of cheering us up.

We must recognize that true beauty has a way of manifesting that which we crave. . If we can see something and accept it as being beautiful we are on the proper pathway of enriching our lives. Follow the footsteps of the great Nyorai who engaged beauty into all they did, thus allowing the infusion of love to penetrate all of humanity.

Beauty may be seen in various different ways. For example, we may look at a tree and like the form of its trunk, or its color, or its leaves. The great maple gives us lovely maple syrup in the Springtime, which tastes so delicious on those buckwheat pancakes.

When we listen to music, let it break into our very core, our heart, for every note of music carries with it a special message for each individual, and for all of humanity as well. Music can be soothing depending on how we go about receiving it. It may tell us something of ourselves if we allow it to, and something about others.

The beauty all around us is remarkable and if we allow ourselves to, there will be magnificence in everything we see, every day as we travel our loving path. If there is something in nature which is not near our home but we know it exists about twenty to fifty miles away, take the trip. It will be worth doing this for something that especially makes us happy. Or, if it isn't possible to travel, then just sit comfortably in a chair and visualize that animal, tree, stream, or anything else in nature which you have always loved.

If one sees another person as being beautiful, then treating the person with love will be an automatic thing. This grows! Once one person is treated with love, treating more persons with love will always happen. The multiplication of this striking process has no end but it does bring an individual to an enriched state, a state of love where love and loving ways discount all else. The individual will clearly recognize, as the great Nyorai of the Age of Innocence did, that love for all of humankind is indisputable and unwavering.

Beauty is everywhere and once this is realized it will help us to see all in a loving way. It will help us to handle day-to-day issues with love or loving ways. It will bring us to a place on our own personal path in such a manner, that we will experience and savor all of our days on this our earthly planet. So, when we honor all of nature and its components, and all other humans on our earth, we see things in a way of our Divine God. When we see a flower, bush, leaf, stream, mountain, bird and all else in nature, it is relevant to admit freely that they too are love, just as we are.

It is essential to have a mission in life, something, that is apart from your daily life. This can be in the form of helping others. It doesn't even have to take on gigantic proportions. Something like showing someone they are respected is a nice gesture. Or, opening a door for someone! Or, complimenting a person on what they are wearing! Or, offering to do something in the form of community work. Or, giving of food or clothing to those who have less. Or, doing numerous kinds of errands for the elderly, such as driving them to the doctors'. There is so much out there, and each person can choose their missionary work based on what they would like to do. This type of mission work leads to personal happiness, love and more love.

It is also important to praise someone for a job well done. Or, to show gratitude at some level when it is warranted. Tell someone they are a nice person, and it is a pleasure to know them. Mention that you like their hair style and its very becoming. Or, if you saw a neighbor plant a shrub in his front yard, say how much it adds to the appearance of the house. That is love!

Forgiveness, no matter what the situation is, is a very powerful tool in creating more love. From the time we came to this earth there are those times which call for forgiveness. We may have gone to a school where the teacher had favorites and you weren't one of them. Forgive the teacher for this! Schools are a place for learning and not to show favoritism amongst students. Perhaps you were thinner than others and there was name calling. Forgive the person or persons who did this. Maybe you weren't able to catch that ball as quickly as others during recess and they laughed at you. Forgive them!

Perhaps your mom or dad didn't understand a situation which made you cry. Forgive them for it. Maybe your mom took the side of the teacher, and you didn't understand why, and it upset you terribly. Forgive her!

When you entered high school some boys or girls may have made fun of your looks, study habits, or lack of social activities. Maybe you didn't like gym but were forced to take it anyhow. Forgive the people involved.

When you graduated high school and went to college or work, there was ridicule of some sort. You found out your so-called friends were not really your friends as they weren't trustworthy. They may have laughed behind your back or made unpleasant comments. Forgive these people.

When you started to date, maybe you believed it would be ever so much more romantic than it was. You found it to be a nightmare instead! Others took advantage of you and then they tattle tailed to others about it. Forgive them for these actions.

If there was abuse in your background, the ramifications

of it stay with you the rest of your life. Counseling helps but memories remain. Forgive your abusers for it will ease the pain. When you were in a relationship and it ended abruptly with hardly any explanation, forgive the person. You found out your spouse had affairs! Even though this is unacceptable behavior leading to separation, or perhaps even divorce, work to forgive him or her. If you both go your separate ways and become involved in other relationships, you will have learned something from the one that didn't work. And, forgiveness will not 'beat you up' internally. It will ease the pain as forgiveness is understood totally by our Divine God and all of the Archangels, and they will love and support you through difficult periods.

If you have children and find there are so many blockages to a loving relationship with them, forgive them, and love them! At some point it will help to bring about harmony to the relationship.

Some of these situations are traumatic! Everyone is encouraged to seek the support of loving counselors, and those in the celestial realms who want to help. Those persons who we feel are the reason for our misery, also need help as they haven't found a beautiful path to follow in life. So, they need all of humankind to show them love as well, until they redefine their lives to a loving way of life.

To be judgmental detracts from forgiving someone, and our own beautiful goal in life, love and loving ways, and brings about other undesirable qualities such as temper, name calling, jealousy, hatred, resentment, wishing someone bad happenings, envy, and anger to mention a few Passion is an important ingredient in living a life filled with love and loving ways. All those wonderful aspects of nature and human existence will continue to fascinate in such a way, passion for life will increase. An individual's entire being will become filled with the passion felt by those who lived during the Age of Innocence. This type of magnificent passion may be acquired if desired! Nothing or no one may stop an individual from discovering it, and letting it become part of life. You will feel this passion to the depths of your being, and love will emerge to enrich lives of those close to you, even the lives of your pets. Passion contributes to a great desire for living life to the very fullest, with the goal being that of helping others to enrich their lives.

Our Beloved Archangel Raphael had such a passion for spreading love across the world, no matter what continent it was, that he visited everywhere possible to spread his teachings. His love for humanity was so strong that he will be on this earth many times during the Age of the Loving Astral and he promises to guide those who need it. Our Beloved Archangel Raphael is truly representative of passion for love and loving ways.

As we mentioned, there are so very many kinds of love and each unite one individual with another. Love in all its precious forms carries a special energy. It is a creative force to attain that which we seek. This kind of love not only cleanses our physical self, soul, and heart, it also cleanses the Earth and creates a new kind of Earth. Some say this new world is upon us very shortly, and, with our help we unite all forces to the highest degree and permeate love into all aspects of life, human, and animal to make this new world possible.

The magnificence of a world in transformation as it is this now is amazing.

To live in a time where the love from the transformation has actually taken hold is something imaginable if we allow our total selves to be involved in the loving conversion of the world. It is in this kind of world where there is a balance between love given and received, and love given and the multiplication of same by one hundred fold.

It is well worth pondering the issue of a loving world. Moreover, it is worth to actually practice what a world like that would be like. In a world of love and loving ways, answers to even the most difficult or sophisticated problems would come to us. It is through the third eye that oftentimes a person may actually see an answer to a problem. One must trust what they see for it is given as a gift from our Divine God and Archangel Raphael.

Some answers may come and occupy the heart area and it is through trust that a person learns to allow these loving answers to come in. There is a definite connection with our Divine God, Archangels, Angels, and others in the celestial realms. At times, those who passed before us may help retain love and loving ways skills to handle even the most problematic issues. At this point, it may be an astute decision to find a comfortable place and try resolving a dilemma utilizing love and loving ways to do it. It need be only a small issue to begin with.

It may be a good idea to just jot down six or eight troubling matters on a piece of paper. Then, look over your list and decide the one that most needs attention. How would you resolve it using love and loving ways? What may come to an individual's mind first is the usual way of solving a problem. Let it be! Don't condemn it or say, "I can't do that," or anything else.

Take as much time as necessary as this first exercise is of great importance as one travels their spiritual path. A loving resolution will come! And when it does, it will bring such beautiful feelings of love and warmth into your heart area. These feelings tend to spread to the entire physical being. When you feel the answer chosen to solve the problem is loving and workable, note the feeling of love will also enter one's soul. It is then the time to try out love and loving ways on your life's issues, concerns, or situations. Remember, it doesn't matter if issues are small or large! In utilizing love and loving ways all issues have the same importance. The first time you initiate using this approach may be the most difficult. From then on, an individual will want to employ it as the results will always be superb. They will indeed have a bravura effect on your life and the lives of all occupying this, our beautiful earthly kingdom. It will put you directly on the path to Joy. It is very important to remember that the individual or individuals you are dealing with may not yet be on a loving path. Be patient with them but firm in your commitment to follow love and loving ways to seek answers or resolve issues. This is your opportunity to be the magnificent teacher, the great Nyorai of our time!

Once you have mastered how to manage all matters with love and loving ways you are on your way to reaching the ultimate, that which is Joy. It is a divine path! Your entire being will welcome the lovely feelings of love deep within you that you have not experienced anytime before. There will be those times of doubt even when you will ask yourself if you deserve it. The answer is a resounding yes. You are a Divine Being living in a Divine world. You have become one with our Divine Creator, the Angels and all others in the celestial realms, as well as all of humankind.

It is your Divine birthright to feel peace, serenity, and tranquility which is a form of love. Slowly, as you take on this practice of love and loving ways you will become totally engulfed in love from head to toe. You will become a model for the goodness of life, and that goodness will spread until it reaches the far ends of our planet. It will extend itself to other planets as well.

Know that an alluring paradise will become yours which with many others like yourself, you will help create. Eventually, all humans will become involved in this process of love. Each human will see only the goodness of life in another human being and thus that goodness or love will grow and grow until All become One in the love of our Divine God.

The energies that will go along with this type of behavior are astounding and will emanate from the heart area. The heart carries so much love in it and when this love is let loose, it is the length of depth of our earth. Our beloved Archangel Raphael believes all Beings will one day walk in splendor for everyone will be endowed with the love of the Age of Innocence. That love was so powerful during those precious times that creating new loving ways of handling problems will be available within the deepest wells of the heart and a person's entire Being. The many new ways which will show themselves in one way or another are through the outstanding partnership with the Divine God.

Our beloved Archangel Raphael believes that all situations are life's advancements toward an enriched life. Your Being will be completely filled with confidence whenever you seek counsel, wisdom, guidance or assistance in handling all life situations. If any hesitation or uncertainty occurs which is not likely, our Divine God, the Archangels, Angels and others in the celestial realms will be there waiting to assist or to come to earth to help. Eventually, through the love process, earth and the celestial realms will merge, each giving the other support and backing whenever it might be needed.

It is essential to acknowledge that each Being began a life on this earth bathed in love. This will allow the negativity surrounding our existence to disappear. It will take time but it will happen. The negativity will turn to beauty and thus that exquisiteness will allow our earth to become characteristic of the beauty of the Age of Innocence where everyone lived their lives in the present now. When this happens, the earth will manifest into positivity and the shared love force energy will work its daily miracles on our earthly planet and it will become infused with love. This loving energy force will carry through space to other planets and galaxies.

With this strong love force energy we will all have the opportunity to think about those effects which the earth doesn't yet have, and create them for the benefit of humankind. So to think beyond the normal range of thought will be possible with love and loving ways. As a matter of fact each individual will be encouraged to think that which is not yet. The Oneness we will experience will allow us to co-create a planet with the potential of becoming a paradise where persons work hard, but also reap the benefits of an enriched life for themselves, those they love, those they know, those they don't know, and all of humankind.

Creation of a better world is by no means left to only a few humans. People refer to them as famous or well known. It is the birthright of each and every human to create that which is beautiful, useful, and loving.

The Divine Plan, or God's Divine Plan, for all of humankind is to better the world and enrich the lives of all inhabitants of our stunning earth. The time for a collaborative effort to build a magnificent Divineness is now, as we are going through the great transformation. It is within the reach of everyone to contribute through love and loving ways, that which will ring out clearly through the centuries to come.

The possibility of utilizing love and loving ways is within the reach of everyone.

When we are able to handle day-to-day problems with love, then we are on the path to living an enriched life. An enriched life brings us closer to our Divine God, and all of humankind. We will then experience the ultimate, that which is Joy.

You Are Love!

You Are Love
– A Loving Meditation™

For this meditation it is best if one is in a reclining position or sitting in a very comfortable chair. It needs to be read to you by someone close to you so that the person receiving it may totally relax and enjoy it to the fullest, and in some way be gifted by it..

You are about to take a trip far away from your home, where life is different as you have always known it; where it is loving. You will first travel and become a part of a small festival. The festival is held yearly and it is near a beautiful temple. The temple is known for its meditative powers and many great mystics have meditated inside this temple or outside, near it. The temple lies directly in front of a huge black rock where it is believed that a Guru of the early seventeenth century defeated a demon. You take the time to think about this situation, how the battle between the Guru and the demon went. It brings you pleasure to know that the demon would not harm any of the townspeople. He is gone forever.

You very much want to go to the Temple. It is not possible for you to go inside as it is locked at the time you arrive there. You say to yourself, "if only I can touch the door of this blessed temple, I would be happy." So you climb the steepness of the mountain where the Temple is. At first, you don't believe you can do it. It is such a challenge. Then, you think to yourself, "how many others have done this?" It was apparent to you that perhaps thousands have made this climb successfully. To be able to touch the doors would be worth it.

You are very exhausted as you begin the climb. It is a mind thing. Your mind is focused on becoming tired but then you change focus. You tell yourself you have a calling to reach the top of this mountain, which in reality, isn't so high at all. With your attitude changed you are able to climb the mountain. You take it easy! You rest and then you move on. You rest again as needed and then move on! In your very heart, you know you will make it to the top of that mountain. And, slowly, you do! Your legs feel some stiffness but it no longer matters! You walk slowly to the entrance of the temple and try the doors. Sure enough, the temple is now closed but you do have the opportunity to touch the temple doors. What beauty! It seems to fill your heart! You are so happy to have made it to the top of this mountain. You sit near the doors and pray. After a long while you take the descending steps down the mountain.

Your mood is that of happiness as you arrive at the magnificent dance festival. The air warms the mountains. The dancers wear masks and beautiful silk costumes to take on the characteristics of deities. You sit down on the warmness of the grass and watch the spectacle. The dancers re-enact the teachings and legends of their inheritance. The flowers grow so generously all over and the scent fills the peacefulness of the valley. You are there on the final day of the festival and receive the blessings of a monument depicting the holiness of the gurus of the region. You feel the sacredness!

The valleys are noted for their beauty. You now enter what may be referred to as a rich kingdom with its art tradition. It is so different from anything you've ever seen before. You take your time to walk, explore the small shops, and absorb the mystical mood of this peaceful area.

You next want to explore what some refer to as a Shangri La because of its inspiring and beautiful mountains which reverbarate loud booms of drums, bells, gongs and conch shells. What an atmosphere, you tell yourself. In this unique area of mystery and supremacy the silk robed dancers leap in a kaleidoscope of color indicating celebration of rituals. It seems so pure, genuine and pristine to you because these festivals represent traditions dating back thousands of years. You sit down and enjoy the rituals to the fullest. It is time to leave but you wish there was more time. It is at that moment you decide you will some day return here.

Now, you are ready to discover the many ancient treasures associated with art, history and legend of the times. You visit a farm and are encouraged to ride a mule. You do so fully confident that the mules are all tame and nothing will happen to you. The farm owner tells you that some times mules are used to get visitors up the high mountains. You enjoy seeing the rich farmland and being one with nature. You know you may be one with all humans and our Divine God. There is another festival to attend which you are told that has great spiritual connotation. The townspeople of the valley all attend; they are mostly farmers and their families. This festival honors the great cranes. There is first a procession, followed by a religious ceremony. The folk and masked dancers perform vigorously and lastly there is an archery contest. All this in honor of the gigantic black crane! Before beginning this journey you have read somewhere that the black crane was the largest bird in the world so this festival interested you all the more.

The townspeople tell you that the black crane is considered to be a supernatural creature.

These birds are referred to as celestial creatures!

It is now time to move on and climb another one of the spectacular mountains of the region. You are no longer weary of climbing mountains for you know that the other side of the mountain is a beautiful flower filled valley with many temples. The air is crisp as you begin this journey. You realize that by the time you reach the other side of the mountain darkness will befall you. The hike feels like a romp on a hilltop and when you reach the top, you see the beauty below just as the sun is setting and darkness is beginning to set in. There are many religious buildings below and you find your way to one small monastery with very unique old style architecture. That is where you will spend the night. The room you were assigned is small and humble. You feel humble as you change into your bed clothing and hit the bed. Before you know it, after hours of deep lovely sleep you awaken to the sound of music. You get up and look out the window. There is so much more you are able to see now. There is a festival going on and it started at the crack of dawn. Many are celebrating with mask dances; the festival is attended by hundreds of people all dressed in their finest clothes. You can't wait to run out of doors and join them. There is food aplenty and you will taste the specialties of this particular village. Everyone is friendly, loving, and caring. They speak of this festival as a spiritual experience to guide them through the year. You love being there! Every second means something to you.

After spending several hours there, your guide suggests moving on. Your guide rents a mule from a village farmer for there is much walking involved. He is used to it but you may not be. As you get deeper into the valley along the mountainside, there are so many different flowers growing; some you have not seen before. You do recognize the azaleas though. They are striking in their orange and yellow colors.

The walk is relaxed. You stop to look at the mountaintops filled with blooming rhododendrons. You have a chance to study the natural flow of the mountains with their natural beauty and magnificent traditions. While in the valley, you pass by a number of monasteries. Your guide directs you to one which is small in size. You go inside through large winding corridors until you come into a room for meditation and prayer. The guide gives you an hour to do as you wish. You want to spend this time in total meditation and this is what you do. It is so wonderful! There is so much to be learned. Before you begin meditating, a monk comes to you and asks if you'd like something to refresh yourself with. You say yes. He returns with a concoction which is very tasty. You thank him and then spend the time meditating. After your hour is up, the monk takes you on a mini tour of the monastery which you enjoy. Then you are on your way again!

This area is so very peaceful you tell yourself: inside the monasteries and out of doors. You hear music in the distance; there is another festival going on. The mystery of the black necked crane comes to a peak as songs, poetry and legend try to explain the existence of this so called celestial bird. The farmers of the valley hold these kinds of celebrations all over. They consider them something breathtaking to behold. It seems that each year they circle a certain monastery. No one ever figured out why this is so.

In these valleys, are precious rivers, sometimes referred to as sacred! There are many species of birds, flowers, trees, and the black necked cranes. You look upward at the magnificent peaks of the mountains. Quite dazzling you tell yourself. You have not attempted to climb the highest mountain and on this trip it wasn't meant to be. You are now going through a forest region which is lush in rhododendrons which grow to tree size. It is getting late and you are now sitting on the mule as you make this last phase of your expedition. On the other side of the forest, the friendly people are in traditional attire. You have found them to be loving throughout this adventure. You feel it strongly in your heart that each and every one of them has so much love to offer. It is without a doubt you feel they do utilize love and loving ways in their daily lives.

The villagers offer you food and drink and shelter. You feel tired as it has been beautiful and all consuming. The food is delicious, vegetarian, and the drink tastes so different; it must be a unique mixture of certain things. You eat until you are totally full. Then, shelter is located for you and you take it easy for the remainder of the day and night. In the morning, you are awakened to a bell the farmers use to send the cattle to the pastures. You love the sound.

After a warm hardy breakfast, you prepare for a trip up the steep mountains. The farmers perform a ritual for you and your guide for a safe trip. You are looking forward to the trip as it is really the first gigantic mountain you will ascend. This is where the mule will help you. It is written that no one may go up this mountain without the assistance of a trained guide and a mule. You have both! After you say your goodbyes to the townspeople, the animals, and the loveliness of nature, you and your guide are off on an adventure you will never forget. You are ready for it! You want this very much! You have a tremendously good feeling about it! The trek up the mountain is a huge endeavor and it is a slow one. There are many steps you must take before reaching a cliff on one of the mountain's ledges. And, your trained guide and mule know that too. Each step is considered to be sacred! You treat it as such! There are delays! You become tired and need water and a rest! Your guide provides this. Once you nearly fall but manage to pick yourself up. Riding the mule was something you weren't used to but at this point this precious animal served you well.

The mule was friendly and seemed to know how humans take to mountains. So, the mule was exactly in tune so that the trip would be successful. And, that it was. When after many hours of travel, you are very tired. Your guide and the mule are chipper! You see this spectacular cliff with a monastery on the cliff. You ask the guide if this is your destination and he beckons a yes. There is something precious driving you to this magnificent kingdom. It is a huge monastery. You want to reach it as soon as possible.

You are there! At the door you are greeted by a monk. The guide tells the monk that you would like to see the monastery. The monk says that only one temple is available on this day though a basic tour of the monastery was possible. It was huge indeed with its gigantic pillars, rooms, prayer rooms, kitchen, dining areas, and bedding areas. The population of this monastery was like a population of a small village. The monk offered you food and drink which comforted your empty stomach.

Finally, you were taken to the Temple that was open to the public on this day and left alone. You were going to just relax and meditate. You were very tired and wanted to stay here overnight. Maybe the monks would allow it. You would ask.

Now, you made yourself comfortable in a meditative position and began your meditation. It felt so good as your body respected your wishes! You knew some different meditative states and found them all to be of great benefit to you. It was always a loving experience! You knew the meditation would restore the energy your body needed. It would dispel all tiredness. There were those times, too, that meditation made you tired; especially your knees and back would become stiff. But, no more! After much work, reading, practice, the meditation you practiced was loving and helpful.

All of a sudden there appears in front of you a celestial being. At first, you believed it was because you were tired. Then, because you were meditating! But, then you knew, it was a celestial being. It was an experience of the eyes and heart and there was no denying it.

What a beautiful Being with bright shining green light all around. Is it an Angel, you ask? You want to have a conversation with this Being. If only a few words, that would be sufficient to make you gloriously happy. There is something sacred happening you tell yourself.

"Who are you?" you asked lovingly hoping the Being will answer you.

A voice whispers "I am Archangel Raphael!" The Archangel comes closer to you and says to you, YOU ARE LOVE!

End of Meditation.

Following this meditation, it is important to remain in a relaxed state for several more minutes contemplating on your spiritual path.

— 11 —

Messages

In addition to working with Archangel Raphael, messages are received from others. In my prayer world, I received messages from Mother Teresa and Mother Mary that I would like to share. One day while I was praying for a long period of time, Mother Teresa came to me, and asked me if I knew who she was. I told her the beauty I saw before me captured my heart totally. "I am Mother Teresa," she softly responded, "I have a message for those who wish to ponder it." I then told her I would be honored to take her message and put it in my next book. The second message is from Mother Mary and the last from our Beloved Archangel Raphael. The messages, as given here, are exactly the way I received them! They are brief and loving!

April 2009

A Message from Mother Teresa

Peoples of the World,

There is a profound time in the making for everyone in the world. It will be a period of purity and rightness like none other in recent eras. This new era which will come upon all of you in an exclusive equal way will tempt your desires to build a fundamentally divine haven. In this sanctuary there will be those who will show their greatest compassion towards others and in doing so, all supremeness will spring up which will entice others to follow.

I remember the day my loving mother gave birth to me. It was always in my thoughts coming out of her womb and doing the utmost for a society which lacked everything. As a tiny little girl I saw the inequality of a double standard system which enriched only the lives of the wealthy. I knew the poverty on the streets of towns and cities in my homeland and as a child, my heart went out to those who suffered. The poverty cannot even be described properly but as a child of five I already knew in my deepness that people were suffering. I constantly prayed! I loved prayer as it seemed to wipe away the tears in my eyes. Yet, the love I had for the people of India and all over the world who lived the injustices of a system which lacked, constantly troubled me.

As a child, my questions about poverty were often dismissed. I was told not to worry about them. It was someone else's problem. The government would help the people who lacked. I knew in my deepness that it wasn't true. I wanted to hug everyone I saw who was rewarded at the end of the day with a mere cup of food. Much of the food was rancid as it was given from those whose plenty escaped from the opulence of their homes. Those who worked in jobs where there was glowing plenty responded to the poor as best they could. I saw this day in and day out. I saw children and old men, and women, swallowing the food as if there would not ever be another cup for them. They were so grateful to receive that which happened their way.

I walked the streets until my shoes wore out and perhaps this is why my growth was so delicate, but it was necessary to do so. In this way, I was able to show my love to those who needed me. And, it was what I wanted to do most in life. It was what I had thought a great deal about from the time I was five until I became a woman. As a child, it was healing the ill which mattered. I always asked myself if these people lay by the wayside because of malnutrition or were they really ill with some affliction no one knew anything about. I trusted my instincts and the Divine Master, God, came to me one night when I was in bed. At first the light was so bright and spectacular, I wondered if it were an Angel. I was never afraid! I somehow wanted this to happen for God to reinforce within me what was so strong.

And, our Divine Master, God, came to me and told me the people of Calcutta need me but that would just be the beginning of my mission. I was delighted in hearing this directly from the lips of our Lord, the one I prayed to so diligently every day and night. God understood and I was happy that at my young age I was embarking on something which would last a lifetime. It was a mission to help the poverty stricken and those who suffered untold illnesses. My life was going to be dedicated to this foundation.

It was real for me and I was drawn to it. No matter what obstacles might be in the way, I would find a way to overcome them and carry forth the work that God wanted me to do.

My mama oftentimes scolded me for wearing out so many shoes and outfits and I told her it was that which I was doing was my little offering to the world. As I got older, my work with the poor increased and I spent practically every waking hour with those who needed me. My studies came easily to me perhaps because I was meant to do this work. When in my teens I would visit restaurants and the rich and ask if they had any leftover food to offer for the poor. By that time, I had a few helpers! I was very open in my requests and even loud at times so that no one wanted to refuse me.

I lived in an era where it was not easy to accomplish one's desires. Even as a nun of the poor and ill, it was a constant struggle to see people you got to love lead such mediocre lives. Yet, they counted just as much as the well known, the rich, and the powerful. I often wished that I could be ten people all at once to propose such a notion all across the continents. Time was of the essence! Lifetimes go by quickly! Scattered dreams may be picked up and rejuvenated to a beautiful rose. It is all possible for we are all children of our God, our Divine Master. Through our love of one another, the greatness of our being is best extolled. This was the beginning of my love story with God and the hungry and afflicted of the world. There is much more of my story to be told and perhaps it will be!

Loved ones of the World, the Era which you are embarking on will give each and every one of you the opportunity to look past selfish desires, and instead, augment that which is most important. There is no greater reward than to be of help to those who need it.

With love always, I am,
Mother Teresa

April 2009

A Message from Mother Mary

My work with Archangel Raphael on healing and teaching love and loving ways is never ending. Your world has undertaken the great and glorious task in the form of alteration, which will change the way each and every person thinks and reacts to situations, be they large or small. The love once known as the pure love of the ages is returning to those who want it so. But, nothing returns exactly in the same manner it was previously. So, now, loved ones, the new era will bring even a greater opportunity for love to be utilized to its very fullest.

Many changes have occurred in your world over the many years gone by since the Age of Innocence. Countless new innovative methods of doing things have been discovered to make your lives easier. This is what you have been told and scores of you believe this as truth. In a sense it may be considered truth for the many discoveries involving machinery such as a washing machine and dryer, do in fact save time and make chores to be done quickly and perhaps even to be considered effortless. With the onset of the internet which contains information of all sorts, an individual may rapidly recognize that which is of interest at a particular time in the current now.

Yet, it is a true and hard fact that so many individuals on your earthly planet have displayed anger, frustration, hatred, jealousy, and other undesirable attributes. Those of you who consider yourselves to be wealthy are by your own admission not in a state of happiness. Those who have special talents, and all humans do, have not taken the time to discover what those gentle talents involve and how they may improve your lives and the lives of those you love and the lives of all humankind. For, dear angels of your earthly planet, it is only through the solemn and sincere recognition that love and loving ways will bring to you that which will enhance your lives is coming very close to your acknowledgement and recognition in this current now. This is because you are about to embark on the greatest journey that ever was. It is a journey which Archangel Raphael most often refers to as The Age of the Loving Astral.

This will be a time when healing one's body will directly come from within as it is true that love heals the greatest of ills. In the application of love and loving ways, there will be far less diseases and illnesses for most of these are caused by the living standards of the current now. As you are on a whirlwind of amazing change and loving feelings toward all, there is already some semblance in your Universe of the air becoming energized with love. If you jaunt in the countryside and enjoy the fields as they grow wild with grass and breathe in the air of this phenomenon, you will realize it is possible for humanity to make this gigantic shift toward an age where what matters most are human beings, not machinery, which many of you believed made your lives easier.

In the realm of what is important, you will find the number one priority to be that of helping and assisting those who still need support until they reach a point where they will have what is necessary to make their lives more beautiful. In turn, these people will help others and the cycle of love will not end until everyone will realize the tender advantage that love and loving ways bring to the world.

I am Mother Mary. I will always support each and every one of you not only because it is my mission but that's what I want to do. I love each and every one of you in the way our Divine God speaks of love. It is an absolute love. It matters not to me what you think, what your past was like, or if you feel there are deficiencies. I only see love when I look at each and every one of you and I want to give you love always.

Like the Nyorai of the great Age of Innocence I want to work with you to help you in any way I can. I will always hear you if you speak to me and in some way I will signal a loving response to you. So, open your hearts as wide as you can and allow the deepness take in all the beauty and love of the Ages. For it will be then that, remarkably, you will be on a significant journey on your earth which will bring you huge contentment
and happiness.

I will love each and every one of you always.
Mother Mary

June 2009

A Message from our Beloved Archangel Raphael

Dear Friends,

I have recently come to earth and worked all over the world in many different occupations including research, agriculture and of course, medicine, both traditional and spiritual. It was essential for me to do this to be able to relay the truth to each and every human being on this, your spectacular earth. I wanted to feel the energies of your world and it is a stunning revelation to be able to say that energies are changing from the unenthusiastic energies to enthusiastic and positive ones.

This, Dear Friends, is an indication that all of you want a better world filled with love and loving ways for yourself, your families, those you know, those you don't know, and all Beings in the world who need love. It is only through giving love to those Beings who have not yet recognized what the transformation will mean that you may consider yourself a missionary of life. They are frightened and need your support, assistance and loving ways to get them through a difficult period after which they will play important roles in the discoveries which will enhance the lives of all Beings, thus, bringing to the forefront the ultimate, that which is Joy.

As I traveled your earthly planet I asked especially to be on routes where the class system was least likely to show success. It was an amazing experience for me to see that in the remote regions, love, one towards another, was beginning to reign and take hold.

What a awe-inspiring experience it was to see this happening.

The transformational state you have all been going through with some difficulty is now turning into a loving one, and it will gently, heroically and lovingly take you to the Age of the Loving Astral. I saw occurrences of this already which were signs strongly visible to the human heart. It nourished the soul. There are still those in some places on your sweet earthly planet where the current now still reflects a past now and Beings think of themselves as agents of control over the people whose lives they touch in those territories. Without a doubt such Beings need to realize that it is only through love and not hateful negativity that much may be accomplished.

There are still those in the world whose efforts ride upon the souls of the very population trying to bring fear, absolutism, and obedience in day to day life. If the individuals living in these areas do not follow this ethic, only brutal punishment follows.

What an attitude of negativity they have brought to this their current lifetime from perhaps another unhappy existence. How they need our constant love and prayers to adjust the thinking from hate to love. It is all possible. And, like the great Nyorai of the dazzling days gone by, it is possible through love and loving ways to uplift the hearts and souls of such individuals who seem to be frightened and are constantly living in a frightened state. This state necessitates their actions to be most drastic for the fear they experience and live is such that, they want it passed onto others.

Yet, we have learned that many have rebelled such despicable actions and have brought down those who offer negativity by offering them love and loving ways. Dear Friends, you are all on the onset of great times in the history of the world. There is nothing which cannot be accomplished under such circumstances. As was said then can be said once again, you are the great warriors whose efforts will bring about such a positive movement that everyone will join in and rejoice.

It is significantly true that much has changed over the thousands of years where love was the answer to All. It will happen again very shortly and you are responsible for it happening. Your love will mesh with those of your neighbors and this pattern will find its way across the entire world. Each and every individual is on an equal scale. There are no class systems benefiting some groups and belittling others. As such inferiority is but a word and words such as hate, aggressiveness, anger, jealousy are valueless as well.

The transformation to a loving world in the Loving Age of the Astral is now in its beginnings. Many of you here on earth have worked very hard for this to happen. Others who worked diligently, may have passed, but will be back to do more work for humanity. Some Beings are still in the celestial realms preparing to come to earth with a beautiful plan of love to expedite. Their excitement chimes across the heavens and sometimes it can be even heard on your earthly planet! You wonder what the splendor is because it makes you happy!

Dear Friends, to those of you on earth now who want to begin to travel a path of love and loving ways, allow yourself to do it in a slow manner with passion in your heart which will surpass all else. Everyone understands, particularly our Divine God, those in the celestial realms and those on earth that embarking on such beauty happens in little increments. Beings should not become discouraged with minor setbacks for those are only learning indications which will help you on your divine path. Slowly and serenely is the way to approach living a life of love and loving ways. Each day will bring you a modicum of peace.

Do not ever be discouraged saying your life was so filled with anger, fear, hatred, and the like that it is impossible for you to embark on a path filled with love and loving ways. This is the farthest from the truth. The truth is that you were born love. You came to this earth as love. You wanted to remain love all the time you have been here but factors prevented you from doing so. You can regain that love which each and every Being wrote into their plan. Each has something spectacular to offer others and all of humanity. Once you decide calmly to embark on the truth and spend the remaining time of this your current lifetime to enrich your life, that of your family, others, and all of humanity, you will have truly accomplished your goal for this lifetime. There may also be written in your plan, special issues which are important to you that you want to work on and these will effortlessly blend in.

Dear Friends, lastly, I must say, do not allow fear to capture the best you have to offer. The Age of the Loving Astral needs each human to be truly themselves. By this is meant it is time now to begin the journey of truth, of love and loving ways which you wanted when you came to earth.

You are Love!

Until we meet again, I am your loving guide,

Raphael

Loving energy fills the pages of this book.
It will fill your physical self, soul and heart.

...... Archangel Raphael

REFERENCES

Anderson, Joan Wester, *Where Miracles Happen: True Stories of Heavenly Encounters*, Guideposts, Carmel, NY, 1994

Braden, Gregg, *Secrets of the Lost Mode of Prayer: The Hidden Power of Beauty, Blessing, Wisdom and Hurt*, Hay House, Carlsbad, CA., 2006

Browne, Sylvia, *Contacting Your Spirit Guide*, Hay House, Carlsbad, CA, 2005

Cameron, Julia, *Blessings: Prayers and Declarations for Heartful Life*, Penguin Putnam, Inc., NY, NY, 1998

Choquette, Sonia, *Ask Your Guides: Connecting to Your Divine Support System*, Hay House, Carlsbad, CA, 2006

Choquette, Sonia, *Soul: Lessons and Soul Purpose*, Hay House, Carlsbad, CA, 2007

Cherry, Reginald, M.D., *Healing Prayer: God's Divine Intervention in Medicine, Faith and Prayer*, Guideposts, Carmel, NY, 1999

His Holiness the Dalai Lama, *How to Practice The Way to a Meaningful Life*, Atria Books, NY, NY, 2002

Holland, John, *Power of The Soul: Inside Wisdom for an Outside World*, Hay House, Carlsbad, CA, 2007

Honervogt, Tanmaya, *The Power of Reiki: An Ancient Hands-on Healing Technique*, Henry Holt & Co., Inc., NY, NY 1998

LaSota, Mary and Sternberg, Harriet, *Hope, Help, Healing with Archangel Raphael and the Angels*, iUniverse, Lincoln, NE, 2007

LaSota, Mary and Sternberg, Harriet, *Archangel Raphael: Loving Messages of Joy, Love, and Healing for Ourselves and Our Earth*, iUniverse, Lincoln, NE, 2003

Leadbeater, C.W., *A Textbook of Theosophy*, The Theosophical Publishing House, Indian, 1914

Moses, Jeffrey, *Oneness: Great Principles Shared by All Religions*, Ballantine Books, NY, NY, 2002

Myss, Caroline, *Entering the Castle: An Inner Path to God and Your Soul*, Free Press, NY, NY, 2007

Newton, Michael, Ph.D., *Destiny of Souls: New Case Studies of Life Between Lives*, Llewellyn Publications, St. Paul, MN, 2000

Okawa, Ryuho, *The Challenge of the Mind: A Practical Approach to the Essential Buddhist Teaching of Karma*, Time Warner, UK, 2004

Okawa, Ryuho, *The Essence of Buddha: The Path to Enlightenment*, Time Warner, UK, 2004

Rinpoche, Tenzin Wangyal, *Wonders of the Natural Mind: The Essence of Dzogchen in the Native Bon Tradition of Tibet*, Snow Lion Publications, Ithaca, NY, 2000

Salzberg, Sharon, *Faith: Trusting Your Own Deepest Experience*, Riverhead Books, New York, NY, 2002

Salzberg, Sharon, *Loving-Kindness: The Revolutionary Art of Happiness*, Shambhala Publications, Inc., Boston, MA, 1995

Salzberg, Sharon, *A Heart As Wide As the World: Stories on the Path of Lovingkindness*, Shambhala Publications, Inc., Boston, MA 1999

Salzberg, Sharon, *The Force of Kindness: change your life with love and compassion*, Sounds True, Boulder, CO, 2005

Tolle, Eckhart, *Practicing the Power of Now: Essential Teachings, Meditations, and Exercises From the Power of Now*, New World Library, CA, 1999

Tolle, Eckhart, *A New Earth: Awakening to Your Life's Purpose*, Plume, Penguin Books, NY, NY, 2006

Virtue, Doreen, Ph.D., *Angel Medicine: How to Heal the Body and Mind With the Help of the Angels*, Hay House, Carlsbad, CA, 2004

Virtue, Doreen, Ph.D., *Angels 101*, Hay House, Carlsbad, CA, 2006

Virtue, Doreen, Ph.D., *Goddesses and Angels*, Hay House, Carlsbad, CA, 2005

Virtue, Doreen, Ph.D., *Daily Guidance from Your Angels: 365 Angelic Messages to Soothe, Heal, and Open Your Heart*, Hay House, Carlsbad, CA, 2004

Walsh, Roger, M.D., Ph.D., *Essential Spirituality: Exercises from the World's Religions to Cultivate Kindness, Love, Joy, Peace, Vision, Wisdom, and Generosity*, John Wiley & Sons, NY, NY, 1999

Wapnick, Kenneth, Ph.D., *Christian Psychology In A Course In Miracles, Second Edition*, Foundation for A Course in Miracles, Roscoe, NY, 1992

....as we lovingly move to the Age of the Loving Astral, it is an opportunity for each individual to think about how beautiful the world would be if we all gave to one another the love that is so plentiful in our hearts. And, in so doing, souls would be nourished1 What splendor to create a world with our Divine God and All, which would lead us to the ultimate, that which is Joy!

.........Raphael!